THE
LANCASHIRE
COOK BOOK SECOND HELPINGS

A CELEBRATION OF THE AMAZING FOOD & DRINK ON OUR DOORSTEP

The Lancashire Cook Book: Second Helpings

©2019 Meze Publishing Ltd. All rights reserved.

First edition printed in 2019 in the UK.

ISBN: 978-1-910863-51-0

Thank you: Steven Smith, Freemasons at Wiswell

Compiled by: Anna Tebble

Written by: Katie Fisher

Photography by: Carl Sukonik (www.thevain.co.uk)

Additional Photography: Matt Crowder, Shutterstock

Edited by: Phil Turner, Chris Brierley

Designed by: Paul Cocker

Contributors: Ruth Alexander, Ceara Gurney, Michael Johnson, Sarah Koriba, Lauren Nuttall, Paul Stimpson, Emma Toogood, Sophie Westgate

Cover art: David Broadbent (www.davidbroadbent.co.uk)

Printed in Great Britain by Bell and Bain Ltd, Glasgow

me:ze
PUBLISHING

Published by Meze Publishing Limited

Unit 1b, 2 Kelham Square

Kelham Riverside

Sheffield S3 8SD

Web: www.mezepublishing.co.uk

Telephone: 0114 275 7709

Email: info@mezepublishing.co.uk

FOREWORD

LANCASHIRE IS A COUNTY UNDENIABLY CLOSE TO MY HEART. I WAS BORN AND BRED HERE, TRAINED AT BLACKBURN COLLEGE AND WORKED IN A NUMBER OF LOCAL ESTABLISHMENTS, INCLUDING STANLEY HOUSE AND FOREST AT FENCE, BEFORE TAKING OVER THE FREEMASONS AT WISWELL IN 2009. THIS YEAR MARKS A DECADE THAT MYSELF AND MY WIFE AGA HAVE BEEN AT THE FREEMASONS AND DURING THIS PERIOD AND BEYOND, WE'VE WITNESSED A LOT OF CHANGE ACROSS THE FOOD AND DRINK SCENE IN LANCASHIRE.

Over the last few years, we've seen a different generation of chefs move up the ranks in Lancashire, all with a similar mindset and keen to achieve similar things, and there's a real sense of camaraderie between us. We're all working towards the same goal, which is to make Lancashire a destination, and with the likes of Mark Birchall at Moor Hall, Lisa Allan at Northcote, Tom Parker at The White Swan at Fence and Stosie Madi at the Parkers Arms, it's a genuinely exciting time to be part of the food scene here.

In previous years, we had some great chefs at the helm with Nigel Haworth and Craig Bancroft at Northcote, Paul Heathcote and Charlie and Victor Yu. They really led the way and spearheaded the whole movement. In recent years, we've picked up some serious momentum and now we're a county bursting at the scenes with quality. And that's not just at our restaurants. We've got an outstanding number of local suppliers, with Wellocks, Pennys Meats, Giles Shaw at Wellgate Fisheries, Simpsons Dairy and Bowland Brewery to name but a few, providing venues like mine with the opportunity to serve fantastic local produce to our customers.

This spirit of collaboration and togetherness over the years has seen the county come together and celebrate each other's achievements, and we're all working collectively to spread the message that Lancashire is a destination for food lovers. I feel lucky to live and work in such a wonderful part of the country, alongside some truly talented chefs and producers.

Steven Smith – Chef Owner, The Freemasons at Wiswell

CONTENTS

WELCOME TO LANCASHIRE

A PLACE WHERE WILD RURAL LANDSCAPES, FERTILE FARMLAND AND GENEROUS SEAS PROVIDE FRESH AND INSPIRING INGREDIENTS THROUGHOUT THE SEASONS.

Welcome to Lancashire, the larder of the north-west, where top-grade farming and creative cultivators deliver all types of vegetables from potatoes and asparagus to exotic mushrooms and some of the tastiest tomatoes. From west to east, the salt flats of the Irish Sea roll gently into verdant hills and lush valleys where sheep, cattle and pigs thrive and even the odd herd of buffalo can now be found.

Along the county's 137 miles of coastline, the 'catch of the day' and delicious favourites including Morecambe Bay shrimps and fish and chips 'on the front' have long been a magnet for foodies. Add to this a proliferation of producers, from sarsaparilla and world class gins to more artisan bakes, cakes, chocolates and cheeses than you can imagine, and you have the type of larder others only dream about. In Lancashire, we have it all.

If you're fortunate enough to live in the Red Rose county, you'll already know this food utopia is on your doorstep. Some of the UK's best pubs and Michelin-starred restaurants happily jostle for attention alongside chic cafés and characterful tearooms. Independent butchers, fishmongers, vintners, cheese shops and bakeries can be found in our towns, villages, on our high streets and in those hidden away places some would love to keep as a safely guarded secret.

That's not us, of course. Lancashire is a place that has always welcomed hungry travellers and those who have chosen to make their home here have been drawn into our diverse and distinctive food culture. We want everyone to share a taste of the county.

Lancastrians will happily chat about a stunning plate of food 'somewhere fancy', talk passionately about a fabulous cuppa and slab of cake that 'hit the spot' and wax lyrical about a farmers' market where we've uncovered a local delicacy. You'll also struggle to find a county as proud as we are of our producers. Seek out these clever makers and they'll be pleased to show you how it's made and just how good it tastes, at source.

Don't just take our word for it! Explore Lancashire's culinary hotspots and buy from local producers, markets and shops. But, above all, experience the delight of feasting from farm to fork, and celebrate the taste of Lancashire.

Bashall Barn

CHAMPIONS OF LANCASHIRE

LANCASHIRE CHEFS HAVE LONG UNDERSTOOD THE VALUE OF PROVENANCE, CHAMPIONED PRODUCERS AND HELPED PUT THE SPOTLIGHT ON LANCASHIRE FOOD AND DRINK.

Inspiration for many of our young chefs, now making waves in the culinary world, came from two Lancashire born and bred food heroes, Paul Heathcote MBE and Nigel Haworth. Paul and Nigel both won coveted Michelin stars for their Lancashire restaurants as well as countless national accolades for their work. Throughout their careers, they championed local food producers including the late Reg Johnson, whose Goosnargh duck and chicken continues to be sought after by chefs across the country. Paul Heathcote MBE and Nigel Haworth have now also been named Taste Lancashire Ambassadors, joining an elite group of Lancashire chefs who have put the foodie focus firmly on Lancashire and will help gain further recognition for Taste Lancashire.

Taste Lancashire Ambassadors

Mark Birchall, chef patron of Moor Hall in Ormskirk, was born in Adlington and worked for a time with Nigel Haworth at Northcote. Before opening his own restaurant in 2017, Mark was executive chef of two Michelin-starred L'Enclume in Cumbria. He was awarded his first Michelin star at Moor Hall just a few months after opening, and his second Michelin star in October 2018. In June 2019 Moor Hall was named Number 1 UK Restaurant in the Estrella Damm National Restaurant Awards 100, voted for by chefs, restaurateurs and food writers nationwide.

Lancaster-born Lisa Goodwin-Allen, executive head chef of Michelin-starred restaurant Northcote, spent many years working with Nigel Haworth and took over the reins when he left in 2017. Her Lancashire roots are present in every dish she creates, along with a passion for using seasonal, locally sourced ingredients. As the first female to win BBC's Great British Menu, she has since become a guest judge on the programme as well as on MasterChef: The Professionals.

Lancashire is renowned for the quality of its gastropubs, and has more pubs in the Top 50 Gastropubs list than anywhere else in the north of England. The chefs leading these kitchens are also Taste Lancashire Ambassadors. These include: Gastropub Chef of the Year Steven Smith, chef patron of Freemasons at Wiswell; Stosie Madi, chef patron of Parkers Arms in Newton in Bowland; head chef Tom Parker at The White Swan in Fence (also awarded a Michelin star in 2018); Chris Bury, head chef at The Cartford Inn at Great Eccleston; and Mark Taft, executive chef at the Assheton Arms in Downham. Parkers Arms, Freemasons and The White Swan brought further recognition to Lancashire with their listings in the National Restaurant Awards 2019, at 38, 39 and 96 respectively. Following an incredible performance and showcase for Lancashire produce on MasterChef: The Professionals, finalist Oli Martin, head chef at Hipping Hall, was also named a Taste Lancashire Ambassador.

Discover more restaurants and pubs at visitLancashire.com

Mark Birchall

DEDICATED
ARTISAN PRODUCERS

WITH ITS STELLAR RESTAURANTS AND MULTI AWARD-WINNING PUBS AND INNS, LANCASHIRE IS A COUNTY THAT PACKS A CULINARY PUNCH. THIS IS THANKS IN NO SMALL PART TO AN ABUNDANCE OF INCREDIBLE PRODUCE, AND THE CREATIVITY AND DEDICATION OF OUR PRODUCERS.

Here in Lancashire, heritage producers rub shoulders with new and exciting businesses, creating everything from craft beer to artisan chocolates and snails to 'hipster' milk, beloved of baristas. Add to that ice creams, coffee, honey, cheese, salt marsh lamb, and not forgetting Goosnargh chicken and duck – widely heralded as the ingredient that began to turn London's gaze northwards – you start to get an idea of the hamper of goodies Lancashire serves up.

We're also a county of reinvention and one of the country's finest cold-pressed rapeseed oils now comes from the fields of Lancashire. Wignall's Yallo is produced on a formerly derelict farm that has been painstakingly brought back to life by a husband and wife duo, John and Clare Wignall. The subtle nutty deliciousness of this versatile oil makes it a kitchen staple, as tasty in a homemade carrot cake as it is in a Michelin-starred restaurant dish.

Of course we're renowned for our Lancashire cheeses too, with our traditional crumbly, tasty and creamy varieties still firm favourites. They are made with milk from Lancashire's many dairy farms, and while cows are a familiar sight across the county, Inglewhite cheese producer Caron Lodge also boasts a herd of water buffalo! Their clothbound buffalo cheese was crowned winner of the Best Speciality Cheese at the International Cheese Awards 2018.

Lancashire isn't just packed with superb flavours and ingredients that set the county apart. It also has the talent and drive to share those artisan brands in a special way. We're home to a dizzying choice of wonderful farm shops, delis and food halls all offering the chance to take some of the best products home. Bowland Food Hall, a warehouse-sized homage to Lancashire food, is a regular pilgrimage for many adventurous foodies. Set inside a formerly derelict mill in Clitheroe, its shelves are fit to bursting with any type of Lancashire food you can think of.

Smaller farm shops, run by families dedicated to celebrating bounty from the county, are jewels in Lancashire's crown. Owd Barn Country Store in Bispham, Saswick House Farm Shop in Roseacre, Bashall Barn in Waddington, Barton Grange Garden Centre and Huntley's Country Stores all serve up a brilliant range of Lancashire food and drink. Many of them celebrate Lancashire's strong butchery traditions where you'll find succulent sausages, black pudding and even Lancashire haggis behind the counter.

Discover more producers and farm shops at www.visitLancashire.com

TASTE Lancashire

Kirkby Lonsdale

SALMON SEA TROUT

SHRIMPS

Morecambe

LAMB

BEEF

Lancaster

GAME

Slaidburn

SALT MARSH LAMB

Whitewell

HONEY

Fleetwood

CHEESE

Clitheroe

KALE CABBAGE

DAMSONS

Blackpool

Burnley

OMATOES

Preston

Accrington

BEER

Blackburn

LETTUCE

SARSAPARILLA

CAULIFLOWER

CELERY

POTATOES

Ormskirk

BRITAIN'S TASTIEST COUNTY!

POURING
WITH
PASSION

JOSEPH LIVESEY WOULD BE IMPRESSED WITH LANCASHIRE'S BLOSSOMING NON-ALCOHOLIC DRINKS MARKET. THE PRESTON-BORN CAMPAIGNER AND REFORMER FOR THE TEMPERANCE MOVEMENT WOULD HAVE BEEN SPOILT FOR CHOICE WITH THE NUMBER OF INNOVATIVE TIPPLES MADE BY ARTISAN COMPANIES ACROSS THE COUNTY.

Companies like Calyx Drinks in Burnley are creating drinks with flower power from healthy vitamin-packed blends made using hibiscus, lavender and camomile. Founded by Raphael Ogunrinde, Calyx is putting Lancashire on an international stage as its products are enjoyed as far afield as Dubai and Chile. In Haslingden, you'll find the last bastion of the temperance movement in Mr Fitzpatricks, a company who offer every non-alcoholic taste you can think of, from old-style botanical brews like cream soda or dandelion and burdock to the inimitable sarsaparilla.

We're not all about abstinence though, with an impressive variety of beers and spirits and a definite current taste for gin. Spend any time in Lancashire and you'll discover that we're a county that turns out some of the best in the world. From humble beginnings in the basement of a terraced house in Burnley, the innovative Batch Gin was awarded Double Gold at the 2018 San Francisco World Spirits Competition for its Industrial Strength Gin. The multi-award-winning spirits can now be found in some of the country's most prestigious stores and bars, with followers eagerly awaiting limited edition varieties.

Head to Brindle and there you'll find the home of Cuckoo Gin, also named one of the best in the world. Made entirely on the Singleton's family farm, using local spring water and carefully sourced botanical flavours, the multi-award-winning signature gin has now been joined by Sunshine Gin following a successful collaboration with local honey producers, The Bee Centre.

Look out for Black Powder Gin in Weeton, winner of a clutch of accolades for their Sidelock and Flintlock Navy Gins as well as a World Gin Award in the Best British Navy category. They're all made and distilled by former farmer, John Loftus, and his son-in-law Tony Dalnas on the family farm. Two relative newcomers – Hoyle Bottom Spirits, who use the brook that used to power an Oswaldtwistle mill, and Goosnargh Gin, who take their inspiration from the Forest of Bowland – are also fast becoming favourites.

We've not deserted our tradition of producing excellent craft ales though, with brilliant beers available from Slaidburn to Skelmersdale. Bowland Brewery in Clitheroe, Old School Brewery in Carnforth and Lancaster Brewery, just outside of the historic city of the same name, are joined by a bevvy of skilled brewers offering drinks to suit every palate. Over in the south we've also got Red Bank Cider serving up the fruitiest of drinks with their tempting choice of ciders, perries and even their own apple juice.

Discover more tipples and thirst quenchers at www.visitLancashire.com

Lancaster Brewery

Calyx

Lancaster Brewery

Brindle Distillery

Old School Brewery

Batch

TIME TO
TREAT YOURSELF

AFTER A MORNING AT THE BEACH OR AN AFTERNOON HIKING THROUGH LANCASHIRE'S SPECTACULAR COUNTRYSIDE, WHAT BETTER WAY TO REVIVE OR ROUND OFF THE DAY THAN WITH A REFRESHING CUPPA AND DELICIOUS TREAT?

You're never too far from a great café, tea room or coffee shop in Lancashire. Cakes, savoury treats, afternoon teas and locally made ice creams are the order of the day, often paired with a brilliant view and something to occupy children as well as adults. On the farm, tea rooms and cafés with views of the milking parlour connect children with the original source of their ice cream. Mrs Dowson's near Clitheroe is one not to be missed.

The café at Shores Hey Farm in Burnley boasts beautiful views across Thursden Valley, where you can visit the many horses and ponies looked after there by the HAPPA charity. The Applestore Café at Wyresdale Park is the perfect spot to combine a walk to Lancashire beauty spot Nicky Nook with an impossible choice of homemade cakes and ice creams as a reward for your efforts.

Coffee lovers will be delighted to see an array of independent coffee shops dotted around the county, who are all obsessive about sourcing, roasting and serving their coffee. Whether you are looking for a quick fix on the go, a leisurely cuppa during brunch or an afternoon catch up with friends, the delicious aroma of freshly roasted coffee beans will guide you to the nearest pit stop. Explore Lancaster's Coffee Quarter: a coffee house revival led by J. Atkinson & Co with their beautiful old shop and The Hall, an industrial chic heaven for coffee lovers from beginner to expert. Their café on Sun Square provides a delightful hideaway off the main shopping streets and boasts one of the city's most stunning Georgian facades and is well worth seeking out. In Clitheroe and Blackburn, follow your nose and you'll find the coffee roasters and tea merchants Exchange Coffee Co serving up perfectly made espressos, americano's and flat whites.

With so much dairy farming in Lancashire, you'll be spoilt for choice when choosing an ice cream parlour to visit. The award-winning family business Frederick's has been making ice cream in Chorley since 1892, and Holdens & Co, which is based in Edgworth and was established in 1929, now boasts a café too, perfect for treating yourself after a walk around the pretty Wayoh reservoir. What makes it all taste even better is knowing the ice cream you are eating has been made using milk and cream from the local cows, and the flavours of fresh, seasonal ingredients.

Discover more tea and cake at visitLancashire.com

The Music Room

Dottie's Wafflery at Samlesbury Hall

Holdens and Co

Breda Murphy Restaurant

TIME TO
DISCOVER
AND DINE

TASTE LANCASHIRE IN A WHOLE NEW WAY AND IMMERSE YOURSELF IN
A GREAT RANGE OF OUR FOOD AND DRINK EXPERIENCES.

Whether a themed cookery course, chocolate making, dining with a difference or a brewery tour takes your fancy, we've got a host of experiences to try and new skills to learn all across the county.

Gin enthusiasts look no further! As a county we're producing a wide range of internationally award-winning gins. Join a local expert as you explore the hedgerows and fields, foraging for seasonal botanicals to create your own blend of gin to take home and enjoy. From the fresh spring water to natural ingredients grown locally, discover how our producers distil their refreshingly smooth, award-winning gins with a variety of tours, tastings or workshops to choose from.

If gin isn't your tipple, we have something for all those craft ale fanatics with a selection of brewery tours providing a fascinating insight into the techniques used to create your favourite craft beer. Take it one step further with a truly unique experience at Lancaster Brewery where you can be a brewer for a day. Brew your own beer and fine tune those skills as you work alongside an award-winning team and Master Brewer. You will soon be an expert on floral, fruity, hoppy, malty or robust ales.

Moving from brewing to baking, our Lancashire cookery schools can help any novice to cook like a pro. Whether you're wanting to whip up the perfect traditional afternoon tea, refine your butchery skills, create a Michelin-inspired dinner party in Northcote style or master the art of chocolate-making with artisan chocolatier Choc Amor at Cedar Farm, there's something to inspire everyone with half and full day courses.

At the heart of our Lancashire food and drink scene is our famous creamy, crumbly and tasty cheese. Discover how our cheese makers produce their award-wining cheese at Dewlay's visitor centre in Garstang. Don't worry, we won't make you choose your favourite as we're confident you will love them all, and you can try before you buy in the Dewlay Cheese Shop!

Of course much of the fun is in the eating and in Lancashire we can offer dining experiences on canal boats, steam trains and in the kitchens of some of the county's leading chefs, from the ultra-chic chef's table at Northcote, where the talented Lisa-Goodwin Allen commands her expert team, to the newest addition of Mr Smiths at the Freemasons at Wiswell, where Gastropub Chef of the Year Steven Smith is the said Mr Smith. Discover more at visitLancashire.com

The Lancashire Cheese Deli

Dewlay Cheese Shop

Goosnargh Gin

Choc Amor

COUNTRYSIDE
CUISINE

A CLASSIC MENU INFLUENCED BY HEARTY FRENCH FOOD AND THE FRESHEST LOCAL PRODUCE IS THE BAY HORSE INN'S CROWNING GLORY, TO BE ENJOYED IN RELAXED SURROUNDINGS THAT SHOWCASE THE LANCASHIRE COUNTRYSIDE AT ITS BEST.

The Bay Horse Inn in the village of Bay Horse was taken on by Craig Wilkinson – the current head chef – and his parents, Mae and Brian, in 1992. They had always liked the idea of running a quaint country pub, and The Bay Horse Inn's setting is a rural idyll that's hard not to fall in love with. Without losing its character, the family updated the building and added personal touches including a mural on the dining room wall of Craig's favourite piece of art. In 2010 Craig purchased the business freehold, and his wife Nicola joined the team in 2015, so there's a genuine family feel which extends to all the staff including Becca, the current front of house manager, and Stefan who started as an apprentice chef and is now a key member of the team.

Views of the dairy farm, homegrown flower arrangements and lovingly tended herbs and vegetables in the pub's garden all reflect the importance of Lancashire's countryside in The Bay Horse Inn's ethos. Craig and his team keep the food menus relatively small because freshness and quality seasonal produce is at the heart of their cooking. He describes the food as classic, influenced by French brasserie style dishes, with an emphasis on satisfying plates that are full of flavour

rather than trying to be fancy. He loves to use Goosnargh duck and chicken, and has a strong longstanding relationship with the supplier which ensures the best of both worlds when it comes to things like sustainability.

As a proper pub, The Bay Horse Inn has a range of bitters which more often than not features Bowland Brewery, alongside a celebration of locally sourced gins including Cuckoo from the nearby Brindle Distillery. It has been named Lancashire's Pub of the Year by The Good Pub Guide, and is a two-time winner of Lancashire Life's Dining Pub of the Year award. Atmosphere plays a big part in these recognitions, which is thanks to the warm welcome from the team and their genuine commitment to the venture. "We love welcoming people for all occasions here," says Nicola, who even celebrated her own marriage to Craig at The Bay Horse Inn. The stone barn outbuilding has been repurposed as a wedding venue with its own bar, and although the pub itself doesn't have rooms, it does have a strong connection to Lancaster Barn B&B which provides beautiful accommodation 'within stumbling distance' for guests!

LANCASHIRE LAMB RACK, RED CABBAGE, HAGGIS, ROAST POTATOES AND HAZELNUTS

"This is a classic dish of lamb and red cabbage that I've reworked a little, inspired by trips to French bistros and brasseries, in particular the Excelsior in Nancy and La Coupole in Paris. I think we produce some of the finest lamb in Europe in Lancashire and this is a dish that reflects its quality." Craig Wilkinson, head chef.

FOR THE RED CABBAGE

I red cabbage
750ml red wine
Splash of red wine vinegar
100g brown sugar
Few sprigs of rosemary
Sea salt
White pepper

FOR THE LAMB AND POTATOES

4 lamb racks (3 bone, French trimmed)
Glug of extra-virgin rapeseed oil
16 mid or new potatoes, washed

FOR THE KALE

Bunch of kale

FOR THE SAUCE

I litre chicken stock
I litre lamb stock
150ml Port

FOR THE HAGGIS

250g haggis
Knob of butter

TO PLATE

Handful of hazelnuts, toasted and crushed

FOR THE RED CABBAGE

Cut the cabbage into eight segments, being careful to leave the stalk in. Place in an ovenproof dish and cover with the red wine, red wine vinegar, brown sugar, fresh rosemary, salt and white pepper to taste. Cover with a lid or tin foil and braise in the oven at 200°c for approximately I hour or until tender, then remove the lid or foil and put back into the oven for 10 minutes to caramelise.

FOR THE LAMB AND POTATOES

Season the lamb to taste with salt and white pepper. Pour a little rapeseed oil into an ovenproof frying pan and place the lamb racks in it fat side down. Roast for 15 minutes in a hot oven then turn the lamb racks over and cook for a further 3 to 4 minutes. Remove from the pan and rest for 10 to 15 minutes for a nicely pink interior. Keep the lamb fat.

Meanwhile, place the potatoes in a pan of salted cold water (just enough to cover them) and bring up to just under boiling point. Cook until they just give a little when you pinch them. Drain then refresh in cold water. Roast the potatoes in the lamb fat, using the same ovenproof pan, for 8 to 10 minutes. Turn them over halfway through to avoid burning one side. They should just be nicely brown and slightly crispy.

FOR THE KALE

Pick the kale leaves, remove the stalks, cut the leaves into bite-size pieces then wash thoroughly in cold water and drain. Blanch the kale in boiling salted water, refresh in cold water and set aside.

FOR THE SAUCE

Place the chicken and lamb stock in a pan with the Port and reduce the liquid until the sauce coats the back of a spoon. Season to taste and keep warm.

FOR THE HAGGIS

Warm the haggis in a small saucepan with a knob of butter, either under the grill or in the oven.

TO PLATE THE DISH

Place the red cabbage in the centre of the plate, spoon the haggis on, then cut the lamb racks down the middle and place next to the red cabbage. Halve the potatoes and arrange next to the lamb, warm the kale in a little butter and lay over the lamb, spoon some of the sauce on and around the dish and finally sprinkle some of the crushed hazelnuts over.

Preparation time: 30 minutes | Cooking time: 1 hour 25 minutes | Serves: 4

THE BUZZ ABOUT
ETHICAL BEEKEEPING

THE BEE CENTRE IS THE HOME OF SUSTAINABLE BEEKEEPING IN THE UK. BASED NEAR PRESTON, LANCASHIRE, THIS PIONEERING ORGANISATION PROMOTES AN ETHICAL APPROACH TO BEEKEEPING AS WELL AS ENHANCING HABITATS AND BIODIVERSITY ACROSS THE UK. IT ALSO PRODUCES DELICIOUS HONEY!

It all started when Kath Cordingley – now a recognised expert in her field – was bought a beekeeping course as a birthday surprise by her husband, Simon. Within three weeks she and their daughter Melissa were absolutely hooked and had bought roughly 100,000 bees! Today, The Bee Centre manages nearly 10 million honeybees in their many apiaries across the north-west and North Wales.

Simon and Kath have drawn upon their professional, environmental backgrounds to establish this multi-award-winning organisation as a national centre of excellence in bee-related matters. Unusual in the beekeeping world for many reasons, making honey is not actually the focus of what they do. They prefer to leave as much as possible for the bees to enjoy. Consequently, this delicious resource is in fact a happy by-product of their environmental and educational activities. Their main interest is breeding sustainable, locally adapted honeybees, based on the native black bee, which are well suited to the Lancashire climate and will pollinate a wide range of flowers as a result.

The raw, unprocessed honeys which they do produce are of a very high quality. Their ethical, low interference approach ensures that this delicious, sticky treat is not contaminated with processed sugars nor chemical treatments. Their sustainably bred bees gather a diverse range of nectars, resulting in honeys which taste and look incredible.

Rather than focussing on honey production to generate income, Simon and Kath have diversified across many sectors. In 2016, they set up their first visitor centre and 'showroom' in the grounds of Samlesbury Hall. Here they developed a range of eco-tourism and education activities which are now being rolled out around the UK. They have also collaborated with carefully selected partners whose high standards and levels of customer service align with those of The Bee Centre. These include some of Lancashire's best producers, such as Brindle Distillery, Choc Amor and Wignalls Yallo.

The Bee Centre also works with landowners and local authorities to create suitable habitats for wild bees, farmers to pollinate crops and corporate clients to improve their environmental impacts. They also run amazing corporate days, based upon their award-winning 'Bee Experience'.

From school children to beekeeping enthusiasts and organisations to the general public, The Bee Centre promotes the benefits of unprocessed honey, ethical beekeeping practices and environmental protection to everyone.

THE MANY WONDERS OF

RAW HONEY

HONEY HAS BEEN VALUED BY HUMANS FOR THOUSANDS OF YEARS, BOTH AS A DELICIOUS SOURCE OF NUTRITION AND A VERSATILE MEDICINE. IT IS MADE BY HONEYBEES, WHICH COLLECT NECTAR FROM FLOWERING PLANTS AND PROCESS IT IN HONEYCOMBS. THEY REDUCE THE WATER CONTENT TO PRODUCE A CONCENTRATED SUGAR SOLUTION WHICH IS KNOWN TO STORE INDEFINITELY, IF KEPT SEALED. IN FACT, ARCHAEOLOGISTS HAVE RECOVERED PERFECTLY EDIBLE 3000-YEAR-OLD HONEY FROM THE EGYPTIAN PYRAMIDS.

Honey provides a balanced diet and source of energy for honeybees as well as contributing to their medicine cabinet. A colony will use around 300lb (over 130kg) of honey in one year, just to keep themselves alive and healthy. If we are lucky, they may even produce a small excess, which we can use and enjoy.

Honey contains a careful balance of over 200 components. This includes sugars (glucose, fructose and sucrose) and small amounts of pollens, amino acids and natural yeasts, as well as B vitamins and vitamin C. There are even trace minerals such as calcium, iron, zinc, potassium, phosphorous, magnesium, selenium, chromium and manganese. The flavour, colour, texture and medicinal properties of honeys are determined by the nectars the bees use to produce them. Consequently, there are potentially as many different honeys as there are flowers and combinations thereof.

The medicinal properties of raw honeys have been recognised for millennia. It has long been known as a cure for hayfever. As a wound dressing, raw honeys can help to protect against infection, reduce inflammation and promote skin growth, thereby reducing scarring.

The antibacterial and antiviral properties make them ideal for combatting sore throats. Some honeys are excellent for calming digestive problems, including indigestion and acid reflux. Raw honey contains antioxidants which support general health and dietary benefits, and the sugars in honey provide a lower GI alternative to processed sugars and can help to stabilise blood sugar levels.

At The Bee Centre, we are regularly amazed to hear reports from customers who have benefitted from this amazing product that our bees produce. Sadly, many of the beneficial properties of honey are lost once it is processed for sale by large-scale producers. Often it has been heat-treated, microfiltered and had processed sugars and water added, ending up as little more than sugar syrup.

To benefit from the incredible properties of 'real' honey, source it locally from a reputable beekeeper and make sure that it has not been processed. To find out more about honey and honeybees, as well as recipes for using honey, visit www. TheBeeCentre.org.

ROOM
WITH
A VIEW

OFFERING SOPHISTICATED CONTEMPORARY DINING WITH ELEVATED FLOOR-TO-CEILING PANORAMIC VIEWS, BERTRAM'S RESTAURANT BOASTS A BEAUTIFUL AND ROMANTIC SETTING, WITH FOOD TO SEDUCE ANY HEART.

Bertram's is a family-run business that has become recognised as one of the go-to culinary and social destinations in the north-west. Its stylish contemporary feel matches the outstanding signature dishes of acclaimed executive chef and director, Spencer Burge, and head chef Gary Entwistle. The result of the team effort at Bertram's is an affordable and sophisticated dining experience in a breathtaking setting. Guests enjoy a delicious and varied menu based on locally sourced ingredients, while dining in front of floor-to-ceiling windows with stunning views of surrounding woodland, set against the backdrop of Pendle Hill.

The restaurant is part of the Crow Wood Leisure resort that is also home to The Woodland Spa – winner of the Global Luxury Day Spa of the Year Award – which both opened in 2013 following a £5 million investment. Nevertheless, Bertram's has a character and identity of its own, from the subtle but elegant styling to the culinary excellence that has seen recipes devised by Spencer Burge feature in the Great British Cookbook alongside the likes of celebrity chefs including Nigella Lawson, Rick Stein and Paul Heathcote.

Testament to its fine reputation spreading across the county, Bertram's has won the much coveted Taste Lancashire Award against some well-established competition, proving that the restaurant is well and truly on the culinary map. Bertram's was then awarded 'Global Winner' in the category of Best Luxury Restaurant at the World Restaurant and Spa Awards, flying the flag for the UK on the international stage. Managing director Andrew Brown and Spencer Burge both travelled to Vietnam to represent Bertram's and collect the award. If that wasn't enough, Bertram's has two AA rosettes and saw even more success in 2019, with two international awards including Best Spa Restaurant.

The people behind Bertram's never take its success for granted, and have vowed to push harder than ever before with the aim of keeping customers happy and eager to return for more. Not allowing complacency to settle in, good staff retention and continuing investment is what sets the restaurant apart. A good example of this investment is the AA accredited five star accommodation which now complements the restaurant's offerings.

BLACKCURRANT TART WITH BROWN SUGAR MERINGUE

The sharp intense flavour of blackcurrants is a lovely contrast to the sweet caramel notes in the brown meringues. Once the tart has set it can be sliced into portions, or if you have miniature tart cases the mixture can be divided to make eight individual treats.

FOR THE PASTRY

225g plain flour

75g icing sugar

1 tsp ground ginger

Pinch of salt

125g butter

2 egg yolks, beaten

25ml water

FOR THE FILLING

750ml double cream

500ml blackcurrant purée

350g sugar

10 leaves of gelatine

FOR THE BROWN SUGAR MERINGUES

3 egg whites

170g soft brown sugar

FOR THE PASTRY

Sieve the flour, sugar and ground ginger into a bowl then add the salt. Cut the butter into cubes and dot over the flour mix. Using your fingertips, rub the butter into the dry ingredients until the mixture resembles breadcrumbs. Make a well in the centre, add the egg yolks and water, then gradually draw the liquid in and knead lightly until the pastry comes together in a smooth ball. Add more water if the dough is very crumbly. Wrap in cling film and chill for at least 30 minutes.

FOR THE FILLING

Meanwhile, bring the double cream, blackcurrant purée and sugar to the boil in a pan while stirring, then remove from the heat. Soak the gelatine in cold water until soft then squeeze out the excess moisture. Stir the gelatine into hot blackcurrant mixture until it dissolves, then cool the mixture until it has thickened slightly but do not refrigerate at this point. Taste and add a little more sugar depending on how sharp you would like the filling.

Preheat the oven to 190°c. On a lightly floured work surface, roll the pastry out to make a circle large enough to line the tart tin, making sure it is an even thickness all over. Press the pastry lightly into the tin, trim off any excess pastry then cover with greaseproof paper and fill with baking beans. Bake the tart case for approximately 15 minutes, or until pastry is golden brown. Remove the baking beans and paper, seal the tart case by brushing the pastry with beaten egg yolk and then bake again for 2 minutes. Leave to cool, then fill the tart with the blackcurrant mixture and refrigerate until set.

FOR THE BROWN SUGAR MERINGUES

Whisk the egg whites until foamy, then keep whisking while gradually adding the sugar, one tablespoon at a time, until the mixture holds stiff peaks. Pipe the meringue mixture onto a baking sheet lined with greaseproof paper. Bake at 120°c for about 1 hour. If possible, turn off the oven after the cooking time and leave the meringues to cool in the oven. This will prevent cracks forming as they cool.

Serve the meringues with the set tarts.

Preparation time: 20 minutes, plus chilling time | Cooking time: 1 hour | Makes 1 large tart or 8 individuals

FROM
NATURAL
ORI-GINS

BRINDLE DISTILLERY HAS BEEN DOING THINGS ITS OWN UNIQUE WAY
SINCE THE BEGINNING, ON A FARM THAT PRODUCES THE INGREDIENTS
AND INSPIRATION FOR THE AWARD-WINNING CUCKOO GIN.

Lancashire is the proud home of a young but aspiring venture which is the only distillery in the north-west of England making alcohol from scratch, using barley and spring water from the land that surrounds it. Brindle Distillery came about when farm owners Gerard and Cath Singleton wanted to diversify their farm to ensure it was profitable for future generations, so along with their son-in-law Mark Long, they converted a big old cowshed and began creating a brand new range of spirits, the first of which launched in June 2017.

Everything is done within the distillery, and uses crops grown on the farm and locally-sourced. Even the distillery building incorporates materials from the farm, giving it a distinctive and striking appearance that also harks back to its original purpose. Mark and his small team hold popular gin-making workshops and distillery tours, which feature tastings and nibbles, in this space. They have also created a bar named The Cuckoo's Nest which opens once a week and fills up with almost 200 people without fail!

There are three gins in the Cuckoo range as of summer 2019, with plans to introduce a rum in the coming autumn and in the long term creating Lancashire's first single malt whisky.

All three gins are award winners: Cuckoo Signature Gin – a traditional London dry gin – won gold in the San Francisco World Spirits Competition, Cuckoo Spiced Gin scooped silver in the 2018 Spirit Masters Awards and Cuckoo Sunshine Gin was Gin Guide's pick for 'Best Flavour' in the same year. Brindle works alongside The Bee Centre in Samlesbury on Cuckoo Sunshine Gin, which is made with natural honey produced on the farm by Lancashire honeybees.

The name stems from local folklore, in which the villagers of Brindle hatched a plan to keep a cuckoo in the village which visited each spring and was believed to bring good farming weather all year round. They set about building a wall around the field where the cuckoo was nesting, but the cuckoo escaped and their plan didn't come to fruition. "Inspired by this wonderful tale, to this day anyone born and bred in Brindle is known as a Brindle Cuckoo, so we felt it only right that we follow in this tradition in naming our spirits, lovingly born and bred at Brindle Distillery," says Mark. The old legend links the distillery back to its agricultural past, celebrating heritage but also looking into the future when it comes to innovating and doing things a little differently.

LANCASHIRE MARTINI

'A reet dapper cocktail.' This Lancashire twist on a classic is sure to get your party started!

Preparation time: 2 minutes | Serves: 1

50ml Cuckoo Gin
15ml extra dry vermouth
1 Nocellara olive (plus more for nibbling)

Stir the gin and vermouth together with cubed ice in a cocktail shaker for 60 seconds. Strain into a chilled martini glass and garnish with the Nocellara olive. Martini is the king of the cocktail world, so we had to produce a version with Cuckoo Gin. We use bright green Italian Nocellara olives as a garnish: sophisticated stone-in olives with a creamy buttery texture. It tastes as delicious as it looks.

SUNSHINE & TONIC

'Hello, Sunshine.' Our fruity and slightly sweet spin on a classic gin and tonic.

Preparation time: 2 minutes | Serves: 1

50ml Cuckoo Sunshine Gin
150ml light tonic or rose lemonade
1 sprig of thyme
2 fresh raspberries
1 strip of lemon peel

Begin by chilling a large balloon glass with ice for 5 minutes. Discard this ice and replace with fresh ice to make your drink. Use lots to make sure the ice doesn't melt. Pour in the Cuckoo Sunshine Gin, then top up with the premium tonic water or rose lemonade. Stir in the garnish of thyme, raspberries and lemon peel. Kick off your flip flops, chill out and enjoy. You've earnt it.

TRADITION
WITH
INNOVATION

SINCE 1932 – FIVE GENERATIONS LATER – BROWNS THE BUTCHERS THRIVES IN THE MARKET TOWN OF CHORLEY, SELLING QUALITY LOCALLY SOURCED MEATS. IT'S ALSO HOME TO THE LANCASHIRE HAGGIS COMPANY.

It was John Brown of Browns the Butchers who initially developed his own recipe for haggis, inspired by old regional recipes. After many trials, he created a lighter and more delicately seasoned version of the Scottish counterpart, which is now award-winning in both England and Scotland with smoked, curried, gluten-free and vegetarian varieties also available. The Lancashire Haggis Company is famous within the county, but now sells its products all over Great Britain too.

Today, John's sons look after the businesses. Tim and Chris select their suppliers locally, using beef reared on a Lake District farm. At Browns, the beef is then dry aged on the bone for a minimum of 42 days to tenderise the meat and intensify the flavour, producing the most remarkable steaks and joints. They are also renowned for their award-winning black pudding. The brothers accidently stumbled across their grandfather's 1945 recipe in the shop attic, and now follow this recipe in all their black pudding products, which include a farmhouse loaf, traditional rings and sliceable sticks. Additional development has delivered the black and white pudding roulade, the haggis and black pudding blend and the firestick (which has as much Scotch Bonnet chilli as the name suggests).

The Browns are passionate about their range of dry cured bacon. Dry curing is completed on site using the oldest and most natural method: by rubbing the salts into the meat by hand. During this traditional process some of the natural moisture is lost, but it adds flavour and reduces shrinkage when cooking. They make unsmoked and smoked back bacon and streaky bacon, as well as limited edition chorizo and maple varieties.

Their methods are often traditional but they also have a continually expanding choice of modern products too, including curries, stir fries and pastries. They continue to vary their sausage range, with the latest additions of pork with stilton and pork with smoked black pudding edging in as customer favourites alongside their established list.

Tim Brown has another claim to fame, in the form of a Guinness World Record for the fastest sausage linking! He managed 60 in just one minute and is featured in the 2018 record book. His son Sam now works full-time in the business too, so that the next generation can continue making the best-loved products at Browns the Butchers and The Lancashire Haggis Company with that winning combination of tradition and innovation.

'THE LANCASHIRE HAGGIS COMPANY' HAGGIS, MUSHROOM AND WHISKY PIE

A delicious but simple dish which will suit the haggis lover, and tempt those adventurous enough to try it for the first time!

1 tbsp oil

1 onion, finely chopped

250g unsmoked bacon, diced

250g button mushrooms, sliced

400g Lancashire Haggis

250ml chicken stock

4 tbsp Scotch whisky (optional)

50g frozen peas

500g shortcrust pastry

Beaten egg or milk, to glaze

Heat the oil in a large frying pan, add the onion and bacon and cook for 6 to 8 minutes until golden brown. Add the mushrooms and cook for a further 2 to 3 minutes. Remove the haggis from the casing, slice and stir into the bacon mixture along with the stock, whisky and peas. Cook everything together for 2 to 3 minutes. Remove from the heat and allow to cool.

Preheat the oven to 200°c. Meanwhile, cut the block of pastry in two, with one half slightly smaller, and roll out the bigger piece on a lightly floured surface. Use this to line a dish or pie plate. Spoon the cooled haggis mixture into the lined dish then roll out the remaining pastry to top the pie. Moisten the edges of the pastry before you crimp them to ensure a complete seal. Trim the edges if needed and use the remaining pastry to decorate the pie however you like. Brush all the exposed pastry with beaten egg or milk to glaze, then bake the pie in the preheated oven for approximately 35 minutes until golden brown.

This is delicious served with mashed potatoes and swede, 'neeps and tatties' or other mashed root vegetables such as carrots and celeriac.

Preparation time: 20 minutes | Cooking time: approx. 50 minutes | Serves: 4-6

A BOLT

FROM THE BLUE

DRAWING ON KNOWLEDGE GLEANED FROM THEIR HERITAGE YET WITH AN EYE ALWAYS ON THE FUTURE, BUTLERS FARMHOUSE CHEESES COMBINES TRADITION WITH INNOVATION TO MAKE ONE OF THE COUNTY'S FAVOURITE FOODS EXCITING AGAIN.

Now in their fourth generation of cheesemakers, the family who run Butlers Farmhouse Cheeses do so with genuine passion and a thirst for discovery. The company was established in 1932, and the recipe still used today for what you might call its flagship product – Lancashire cheese, of course – was first dreamt up in 1969 by Jean Butler, whose daughter Gill and grandsons Daniel and Matthew make up the core team of the business today. Her recipe isn't the only thing they've brought with them out of the rich vein of cheesemaking history in the family. Traditional open vats and handcrafting at each stage of the process means the curds are handled gently, resulting in a more open texture and a cheese that eats and melts beautifully.

Butlers now uses these techniques to produce more than a dozen varieties of hard, soft and blue specialty cheeses, allowing them to create the perfect cheeseboard. The flagship hard cheese is the tried and tested Tasty Lancashire, gold-award-winning Blacksticks Blue is the go-to British Blue cheese and Kidderton Ash goat's cheese completes the trio, offering a soft and goat's cheese in one. 2018 saw the launch of Button Mill, the newest creation to date, which is a soft and indulgent camembert-style cheese that is stocked in Booths and Waitrose. For the Butlers, their growing success is down to the care and forward-thinking that goes into every single cheese made on the farm. "As a family and a company we have innovation at heart," explains Matthew, "and we love to explore new ways to make cheese an experience, not just something everyday."

Butlers sources all its milk from within a ten mile radius, two thirds of which actually comes from the dairy farm across the road which is owned by Gill's brother, and goat's milk from a herd looked after by Nicola, Matthew and Daniel's cousin. All this goes straight from the Lancashire fields into three mini dairies where Butlers Farmhouse Cheeses are produced. Not making vast quantities means quality is always first and foremost, and although they have expanded since the family began their cheesemaking venture, the old ways of doing things are still held close to their hearts. These are absolutely cheeses for the future, however, with quirky packaging and a story behind each variety that promises you an adventure with every bite!

BLACKSTICKS BLUE

People often don't understand how to use blue cheese in cooking. In many cases though, when working with something like Blacksticks Blue, you can simply replace the specified cheese in your recipe and add a different dimension to your dish: all you need is a bit of bravery!

Blacksticks Blue is a creamy and mellow cheese at heart, with blue veins running through to give it that bite you expect from blue cheese. It melts extremely easily and provides a nice zip of colour thanks to its bright orange hue. Adding Blacksticks Blue into a recipe will undoubtedly create new flavours and sensations; it's not for every occasion but cooking is all about experimentation and discovery. The joy of Blacksticks Blue is that it will react just like good cheddar with a totally different flavour. We make our cheese the old fashioned way, which is why it melts so well. The texture is open as the cheese hasn't been squashed in (we hand fill our moulds) and over many years of experience we have learnt to create the very best cheeses for melting.

We've created a few dishes to give you some inspiration, so next time you have friends over, surprise them with a bit of Blacksticks Blue. If you aren't in the mood for cooking it makes a great cheese on toast and the most amazing cheese and pickle sandwich too.

CHEESE SCONES

Cheese Scones are quick and easy to rustle up: simply switch cheddar with Blacksticks Blue and away you go. We recommend adding a pinch of paprika then giving the tops of the scones a milk wash and a good sprinkling of cheese for added colour and flavour.

CHEESE & PINEAPPLE ON STICKS

Cheese & Pineapple sticks just grew up! Blacksticks Blue is unbelievable when served with sweet foods – pineapple is a perfect partner with its sharp acidity – and this is a great way to add some fun to any buffet.

CHEESE STRAWS

Blacksticks Blue cheese straws are the best; the extra flavour in the cheese gives the straws a lovely mature flavour which is difficult to achieve with cheddar.

CAULIFLOWER CHEESE

Another classic given a Blacksticks twist. Simply replace the cheddar in your recipe and create a great accompaniment to any meal. Be sure to sprinkle a good helping of cheese on top for a crispy coating.

BLACKSTICKS BLUE JAM TARTS

These are inspired by our cheese grader Bill, who loves Blacksticks Blue with blackcurrant jam. Make your tarts as usual, add the blackcurrant jam – be sure not to overfill the tarts though – and sprinkle with grated Blacksticks Blue before putting them in the oven. The result is a sweet yet sharp starter or dessert that has a lovely hint of salt, sure to get the tastebuds going.

COME INN

FOR A TASTE

THE CARTFORD INN, AN OUTSTANDING COUNTRY INN AND RESTAURANT, AND TOTI IT'S SHOP AND DELICATESSEN, SHARE A FAMILY AND FRESH APPROACH TO FOOD, DRINK, DESIGN AND HOSPITALITY IN LANCASHIRE.

The Cartford Inn, in the hands of Patrick and Julie's family and team since 2007, has certainly evolved enormously. With Patrick's strong food and beverage background and his origins from Bordeaux in France. Julie's eye for eclectic and beautiful interior design, and her love of art, with a dedicated team led by Chris Bury in the kitchen and Danny Smythe in front of house, they have transformed a rundown pub into a unique and excellent hostellerie. One that showcases a restaurant with two AA rosette, listed in the Estrella Damm Top 50 Gastropubs in Britain, and a wide range of luxury accommodation, rated 5 star gold by both Visit England and the AA. The seasonal menu combines a range of creative dishes and pub classics, all perfectly executed, using the best of local ingredients, fresh fish from the port of Fleetwood, meat from nearby farms, locally foraged produce, and herbs and vegetables from their own allotment by the river in season.

In 2015, Patrick and Julie's daughter Jean ,set up an on-site shop and delicatessen named TOTI 'Taste of the Inn'. Fresh produce including sourdough bread and patisseries are made in-house or sourced from Lancashire suppliers. The shelves are full of unique, fine products from France, Italy and Spain. Jean is growing the selection of own-brand products such as 'Green Gold' a wild garlic pesto, wild-flower honey and handmade chocolates from a local chocolatier with a view to start an online shop in the near future.

TOTI also offers a small lunch menu with favourites such as the incredible French onion soup, great healthy salads and the TOTI choux bun, an indulgent choux pastry filled with pastry cream, Bourbon caramel and topped with hazelnut buttercream which Jay Rayner mentioned in his review for the Observer as a contender for dessert of the year.

The Cartford Inn also offers private dining facilities for special occasions and for their own Supper club, special tastings and exhibitions by local artists.

Their newest addition is a unique space dedicated to art, a creative hub filled with crafts and gifts. It is also a space where niece Tanicia Hayton has set up her own jewellery workshop.

CHILLED WATERCRESS SOUP WITH CHARGRILLED ASPARAGUS AND TRUFFLE EGGY BREAD SOLDIERS

A refreshing recipe from our spring menu using local vegetables such as Preston watercress and Formby asparagus, combining the rustic and comforting texture of eggy bread with the rich flavour of fresh truffle.

FOR THE CHILLED WATERCRESS SOUP

100g potato
2 sticks of celery
1 onion
1 leek
1 clove of garlic
Knob of butter
1 litre vegetable stock
200g watercress
Salt and pepper

FOR THE EGGY BREAD SOLDIER

1 thick slice of sourdough bread
2 eggs
Splash of milk
1 truffle

FOR CHARGRILLED ASPARAGUS

8 spears of fresh asparagus
Olive oil
Sea salt

FOR THE CHILLED WATERCRESS SOUP

First peel and finely chop the potato, celery, onion, leek and garlic. Sweat all the vegetables with a knob of butter in a saucepan over a medium heat, then add the stock and cook until the potatoes are soft. Blitz the mixture in a high-powered blender and add the watercress while it blends. Pour the soup into a shallow tray and chill as quickly as possible to retain the vibrant colour. Season to taste with salt and pepper before serving.

FOR THE EGGY BREAD SOLDIERS

Heat a knob of butter in a frying pan while you whisk the eggs with a splash of milk. Cut the bread into 'soldiers' and soak a piece in the egg and milk mixture. Transfer into the hot melted butter and cook on all sides until golden. Repeat with all the soldiers.

FOR THE CHARGRILLED ASPARAGUS

Snap off the woody ends of the asparagus spears. Rub the spears with olive oil and grill them for 3 minutes, turning half way through. Add a touch of sea salt.

TO SERVE

Pour a little of the soup into each of the bowls. Place the eggy bread on side plates and use a fine grater to dust the soldiers with truffle. Add the asparagus and serve straightaway.

Preparation time: 20 minutes | Cooking time: 5 minutes | Serves: 4

BLOOD ORANGE TART
AND LANCASHIRE PARKIN ICE CREAM

*Our take on the classic lemon tart, using seasonal produce and a taste of
Lancashire. The combination of luxuriously smooth filling, parkin spices and bitter
orange is irresistible. Enjoy!*

FOR THE SWEET PASTRY

125g butter, at room temperature

125g icing sugar

3 tbsp double cream

2 free-range eggs, beaten

350g plain flour

FOR THE BLOOD ORANGE FILLING

5 blood oranges

9 free-range eggs

390g caster sugar

250ml double cream

FOR THE LANCASHIRE PARKIN

225g plain flour

½ tsp salt

1 tsp bicarbonate of soda

2 tsp ground ginger

1 tsp ground cinnamon

1 tsp mixed spice

110g pinhead oatmeal

175g dark muscovado sugar

115g butter, plus extra for greasing the tin

3 tbsp golden syrup

115g black treacle

150ml milk

1 beaten egg

FOR THE SWEET PASTRY

Cream the butter and icing sugar until pale and fluffy then stir in the double cream and beaten egg. Add the flour in small amounts, mixing until it all comes together as a uniform dough. Rest the pastry in the fridge for 1 hour. You can make the parkin during this time.

Roll the chilled pastry out to 2-3mm thickness and line a greased 26cm tart mould. Refrigerate for 30 minutes, then blind bake at 160°c for 10 minutes. Remove the beans and bake for a further 20 minutes, then leave the pastry case to cool.

FOR THE BLOOD ORANGE FILLING

Zest and juice the oranges into the same bowl, so all the oils from the skin go into the mix, as these hold the most intense flavours. Whisk the eggs and sugar together then add the juice and zest. Pour the cream gradually into the mixture, stirring at all times. Leave to rest for 20 minutes. Skim off air bubbles that have formed on the top with a spoon or alternatively use a blowtorch to pop them.

Place the cooled pastry case in a preheated oven at 130°c then carefully pour the filling in until the tart is full to the brim. Close the door slowly, being careful not to knock any mixture over the sides. Bake for 25 minutes until the filling just wobbles in the middle. It will firm up when cooling down. Cover with icing sugar and blowtorch if you like to give colour and a crisp topping. Slice with care and serve with a scoop of your Lancashire parkin ice cream.

FOR THE LANCASHIRE PARKIN

Grease a loaf tin with a little butter. Sift the flour, salt, bicarbonate of soda and spices into a bowl then stir in the oatmeal and sugar. Melt the butter, syrup and treacle in a pan and whisk until emulsified, then cool to room temperature. Whisk in the milk and egg, then stir this mixture into the dry ingredients. Pour the cake batter into the loaf tin and bake for 40 to 50 minutes at 180°c.

Making your own ice cream is tricky, so if you don't have the tools or the time, buy a quality vanilla ice cream, leave it out of the freezer to soften slightly, then swirl through some crumbled parkin.

Preparation time: 30 minutes, plus 2 hours resting and chilling | Cooking time: 1 hour | Serves: 8

SMALL
BUT
MIGHTY

CHOC AMOR IS A MANUFACTURER OF "FIENDISHLY GOOD CHOCOLATE" THAT PROUDLY STANDS OUT FROM THE CROWD THANKS TO ITS UNIQUE FLAVOURS AND GREAT QUALITY CHOCOLATE WHICH IS ETHICALLY SOURCED.

Established in 2012 by husband and wife team Paul and Jacqui Williams, Choc Amor is a small but mighty producer of flavoured single origin chocolate. As one of only six in the UK to be crowned world winners at the 2019 International Chocolate Awards amongst many other accolades, the company has thrived since its beginnings in the owners' kitchen. Paul was made redundant during the recession, and decided that if he had to create his own job, it should follow his passion for food. The idea came from an article on chocolate making, and after attending a two day course Paul has been hooked ever since.

Choc Amor's slabs are flavoured with anything that might have potential, whether that stems from inspiration striking or customers asking for something that hasn't been created yet. The small batch production uses natural ingredients that are free from preservatives, like essential oils and spices, in combination with Colombian 'couverture' chocolate which contains higher proportions of cocoa butter and is essentially some of the best quality chocolate in the world. The beans are harvested, fermented, dried then roasted to begin the transformation into chocolate. Local sugar and extra cocoa butter are added, making all the ingredients fully traceable.

In 2018 Paul and Jacqui visited cocoa plantations in Colombia and were struck by the passion of the farmers and the cocoa they were growing. Colombian cocoa has received the distinction of 'Cocoa Fino de Aroma' from the International Cocoa Organisation, a title given to only 8% of the world's cocoa. Through their cocoa research facility in Colombia, Luker Chocolates train farmers from all over the country so that they can improve their yield, profits and livelihoods. The company also supports the welfare and development of local communities and schools, all of which gives Choc Amor a product that the team can say, hand on heart, is ethically sourced and 100% sustainable.

Their journey began at farmers' markets and food festivals across the county, which are still great places to try and buy Choc Amor products, but the company now has its very own chocolate studio and shop at Cedar Farm in Mawdesley where you can talk to Paul, Jacqui or Judith. This offers visitors a completely different buying experience in a very friendly and relaxed environment. As some of the flavours are a little different, such as Orange Jalfrezi or Chilli Cappucino, the packaging even informs people how to eat the chocolate, to get the most out of each bite. As Paul puts it, Choc Amor is "trying to change people's perception of chocolate one mouthful at a time."

SQUIDGY CHOCOLATE BROWNIES

*What could be better than a really good chocolate brownie with an intense flavour,
a slightly crisp top and a gooey centre? Why not try adding one of the following
as a variation on the recipe below: salted caramel sauce, Morello cherries, toasted
pecans or a pinch of sea salt. Simply delicious!*

280g butter

280g dark chocolate (use the best quality you can; we've used our house 61% dark chocolate)

130g plain flour

60g unsweetened cocoa powder

375g caster sugar

4 large eggs

Preheat the oven to 160°c and line a brownie tin (35 by 20cm) or a similar sized baking tin with baking parchment.

Melt the butter and chocolate together slowly over a gentle heat. You can use a microwave, but be sure to do it in 30 second blasts and stir between each blast, or you could burn the chocolate. Set aside to cool.

Sieve the flour and cocoa powder together into a separate bowl. Whisk the caster sugar and eggs together until thick and creamy in a large bowl, then pour the cooled chocolate mixture into this and fold together with a rubber spatula. Sift the flour and cocoa again, straight into the mixture this time, and gently fold in until everything is just combined. Don't overmix the batter.

If you want to add any extra flavours and ingredients, you can add them at this stage by gently stirring them through the batter. Or, you can simply add them to the batter in the tin and gently press them down into the mixture.

Pour the finished brownie batter into your tin and bake for 25 to 30 minutes. They may need an extra 5 minutes if the mixture is too wobbly in the centre. Resist the temptation to eat them immediately and let the brownies cool completely, preferably overnight.

Turn the cooled brownies out onto a chopping board and cut into 16 pieces. These will keep in a sealed container for up to 2 weeks, or can be frozen.

Eat them cold if you can't wait any longer, or serve slightly warmed with clotted cream and berries. Enjoy!

Preparation time: 20-25 minutes | Cooking time: 25-35 minutes | Makes 16

'FIENDISHLY GOOD' CHOCOLATE TRUFFLES

Truffles are, or should be, the essence of chocolate concentrated in one bite. This is a no-fuss recipe for smooth, silky, creamy little bites of heaven which just melt in the mouth. They may look rather ordinary but they have hidden depths. Enjoy!

70ml double cream

40g light muscovado sugar

25g unsalted butter softened

Pinch of salt

110g dark chocolate (we use our house 61% dark chocolate, but why not play around with different chocolates to find the flavour you prefer)

Cocoa powder, to dust

Line a 15 by 9cm baking tray with cling film so that it overhangs the sides slightly, or use a similar size foil tray.

In a small saucepan, heat the cream, sugar and butter over a gentle heat until it starts to boil. Turn down the heat and allow to simmer for 1 minute. Ensure the sugar has completely dissolved as this will kill off any bacteria which may be present in the cream or butter, and makes sure your truffles will have a longer shelf life. You can use a microwave but only in 30 second blasts, stirring between each blast. Three times should do it. When everything has completely melted using either method, take the pan off the heat, add a pinch of salt and leave to cool for 5 minutes.

Break the chocolate into small pieces, put them into a heatproof bowl and melt slowly in a microwave, again only with 30 second blasts, or a bowl set over hot water.

Combine the cooled cream mixture with the melted chocolate. Stir until smooth and glossy, but don't overmix as it will split. Pour into your prepared tin and refrigerate until set; a minimum of 2 hours or preferably overnight.

Remove the tray from the fridge and use the cling film to lift the set truffle mix onto a chopping board. Cut into 24 bite-size pieces. Dust your fingertips with cocoa powder and gently roll the truffles in it, smoothing the edges and making sure each truffle is well coated. Don't handle the truffles too much as they will melt.

Your truffles are now ready to eat. These will keep in the fridge for up to 7 days, ready for any simply yet elegant dinner party!

Preparation time: 10 minutes | Cooling time: 2 hours minimum, ideally overnight | Makes 24 bite-size truffles (not gobstoppers!)

A FEAST OF A FESTIVAL

CLITHEROE FOOD FESTIVAL BRINGS QUALITY PRODUCE, HEAVENLY FOOD AND EXCITING ENTERTAINMENT TOGETHER IN THE HISTORIC LANCASHIRE TOWN.

Hailed as one of the best food festivals in the UK, Clitheroe Food Festival is an annual event which takes place in the market town of Clitheroe against the backdrop of its historic castle. It's a great showcase for the town which attracts thousands of people on the day! A variety of events spring up on the same day around Clitheroe, including a Pudding Fest at St Marys Hall, a craft fair at Platform Gallery and a scarecrow festival on neighbouring streets led by residents to raise money for the local food bank.

Organised by Ribble Valley Borough Council, the festival hosts a huge selection of delicious local produce and culinary talent; it has become well known for its dedication to the county's best food and drink, and the organisers take great care to keep it that way. Producers are screened for quality and the festival regularly features many with a national reputation such as Choc Amor, Fatjax Chutney, Leagram Organic Dairy and Port of Lancaster Smokehouse.

With over 100 exhibitors offering a heavenly array of food – from smoked salmon and hog roast to scrumptious pies and locally reared beef or delicious ice cream to gingerbread and chocolates – there is something to tempt everybody, and a fine selection of craft beers, ciders, spirits and wines to wash it all down with. Local producers offer a series of tastings on the day, including wine by Barrica Wines, chocolate by Choc Amor and Cuckoo Gin gin by its creator Brindle Distillery.

And if the food and drink isn't enough, the event also dishes up a huge dollop of street entertainment. Regulars include the plate-flipping and napkin-sculpting slapstick of the Comedy Waiters, the popular Mad Science with madcap demonstrations and hands-on activities, and a fun fair in the castle grounds. After the festival, celebrations continue down at Holmes Mill, the site of Bowland Brewery where live music is played into the evening. There is also an evening of live music at The Grand, the town's amazing music venue, where musicians who have played on the festival's main stage perform.

With free fun for all the family and of course plenty of fantastic food and drink, Clitheroe Food Festival truly is a day not to be missed!

Further details are available at clitheroefoodfestival.com.

A FOODIE'S HEAVEN

OFTEN REFERRED TO AS THE FOOD CAPITAL OF THE NORTH, RIBBLE VALLEY PLAYS HOST TO A MOUTH-WATERING ARRAY OF FOOD EXPERIENCES. DISCOVER AN ABUNDANCE OF AWARD-WINNING PLACES TO EAT AND DRINK, EACH SET WITHIN THE STUNNING LANDSCAPE OF THE REGION.

Ribble Valley is at the very centre of Great Britain, and much of the region is designated an Area of Outstanding Natural Beauty. What better backdrop for amazing food experiences? From cosy cafés and tearooms to gastropubs, contemporary mill conversions and a Michelin-starred manor house, there are flavours of the world to be discovered, from authentic Indian to award-winning Cantonese. Grace Dent of The Guardian is a firm admirer, saying "the magical Ribble Valley, somewhere between Lancashire and the southernmost edge of the Yorkshire Dales, hides in plain sight as Britain's finest jewel for the tourist-who-does-dinner."

Great countryside and fine food are the key ingredients of a popular initiative in Ribble Valley. Walks with Taste is a selection of walks through some of the area's most spectacular countryside, each using a local food enterprise as the starting point. The walks feature self-guided routes with maps and descriptions, and offer different distances, durations and terrains to ensure there is something for all tastes and abilities. Walking is a great way to keep fit and work up a healthy appetite, ready for a tasty welcome back at a local inn, café or restaurant. Individual walks are available from participating businesses, and whole sets are available from the Platform Gallery and Information Centre in Clitheroe, or can be downloaded from www.visitribblevalley.co.uk.

Ribble Valley is renowned for the quality of its food, with much of the produce being made at its heart. The suppliers of these artisan products are passionate about creating the best food and drink, available on our doorstep. Much of the locally sourced, hand-reared produce from Ribble Valley is available in local shops, and is showcased at the annual Clitheroe Food Festival, now one of the country's major food events, when the town centre is taken over by an array of culinary stalls – all offering tasteful delights – and is the perfect opportunity to experience the true tastes of Ribble Valley.

Food is so inherent to the culture of this area that we have created a dedicated website where you can discover what is made locally, and all the great places to eat. It also introduces you to the places where local food can be purchased. Go to www.ribblevalleyfoodheaven.com to learn more about our wonderful food experiences.

THE BEST
BANGERS IN TOWN

COWMAN'S FAMOUS SAUSAGE SHOP HAS BUILT UP A DESERVED REPUTATION ACROSS THE COUNTY FOR ITS SIGNATURE SAUSAGES, AS THE NAME SUGGESTS!

The business, which stands in pride of place in a listed building in the heart of Clitheroe, was originally owned by the Cowman family. It was taken over by Ted Cowburn in the 1950s and was then handed down to his son, Cliff. The butcher's shop branched out during the 80s thanks to Cliff who spotting a niche market for inventive sausages, pioneered the use of top quality meat instead of using the by-products of butchery which was the norm. The shop today stocks an impressive 75 varieties of sausage, with additional varieties available during the festive seasons. In addition to their extensive range, the legendary butchers offer the full range of products you would expect to find in a quality Lancashire butchery.

In May 2015, Cliff retired and handed down the business to his long-standing employees, Paul and Nick, who between them have worked on the premises for over 25 years, and in turn are training their apprentice Mark. They describe finding the inspiration for new flavours as a "team effort" and are often given flavour suggestions from family members, staff, friends and of course their loyal customers. Pickle and Cheese, Smoked Garlic with Red Wine and Cajun Pork are just some of the delights on offer, sitting alongside some more hearty flavours such as Wild Boar and Black Pudding with Mead. There really is a flavour combination for everyone! The recipes are all developed above the shop, with family members offering the first taste test.

The business is known far and wide, and even enjoyed a very special visit from His Royal Highness the Prince of Wales in 2017, which really put the business and the historic town on the food map! Cowman's has won awards of national recognition over the years, including Best Breakfast Sausage, numerous gold awards for quality and flavour, and local accolades including Best Small Business two years in a row at the Ribble Valley Business Awards.

Paul and Nick, along with many of the members of staff, have grown up in the town, and describe Clitheroe and the surrounding Ribble Valley as a real food lover's paradise, with local, quality produce at the core. The well-known business holds great pride in their unique position amongst the local community, choosing to stay in the area and ensuring the whole team continue to show their dedication and love for quality Lancashire produce.

HEARTY HOMEMADE COWMAN'S CHILLI

A quick and easy family friendly recipe with a sausage twist!

1 large white onion

1 red pepper

2 cloves of garlic

Slosh of olive oil

10 Cowman's sausages (plain pork or any flavour you fancy)

Pinch of salt and pepper

2 tsp paprika

2 tsp ground cumin

1 tsp dried chilli flakes

1 tbsp tomato purée

1 tin of chopped tomatoes

½ a beef stock cube

1 tin of kidney beans, rinsed

A few dashes of Worcestershire Sauce

TO SERVE

3 tortilla wraps

Natural yoghurt

Handful of chopped chives

Preheat the oven to 200°c (if you wish to make the homemade nachos). Chop the onion and pepper and finely chop the garlic. Heat some olive oil in a large frying pan or use a wok for a larger surface area. Add the onion, pepper and garlic and fry until slightly softened, usually for about 5 minutes.

While this is cooking, skin the sausages by running a knife down the length of the sausage, peeling off the skin and throwing it away. I usually roughly chop the meat just to break it up before adding it to the pan.

Cook for 5 minutes then season with salt and some pepper if you wish, followed by the paprika, cumin, chilli flakes and tomato purée. Stir for a further minute then add the tin of tomatoes. Drop the half stock cube into the tin and half fill with boiling water (this ensures you get all the tomato juice and saves on washing up). Once the stock cube has dissolved pour the mixture into the pan. Be careful as the tin will get hot! Add the kidney beans and Worcestershire sauce and stir them through the mixture.

Simmer for 10 to 15 minutes, stirring occasionally, until the sauce is nice and thick. Taste and add more chilli or paprika if you're feeling brave.

If you are making the nachos, once the chilli is simmering cut each tortilla into eight triangles, lay them flat on a baking tray, ideally not overlapping too much, then drizzle with olive oil or use an oil spray. Season with salt and pepper then cook in the preheated oven for about 5 minutes, but keep an eye on them as they can burn quite easily.

Serve the chilli with rice, a handful of nachos, a dollop of yoghurt and a sprinkling of chives. Enjoy!

Preparation time: 15 minutes | Cooking time: approx. 30 minutes | Serves: 4

ENJOYED

AGAIN AND AGAIN

ENCORE HAS ONLY BEEN OPEN A SHORT TIME BUT HAS MADE A BIG IMPRESSION ON THE FOOD AND DRINK SCENE IN CHORLEY WITH ITS UNIQUE APPROACH TO EATING OUT IN LANCASHIRE.

In 2018 the brand new Encore began to build up a following thanks to a detail-led ethos that is ultimately designed to create the best restaurant experience possible. After managing a previous business in the same venue for two years, Gareth Tebay established his own restaurant in Chorley and brought his philosophy on great hospitality to life with a team of passionate professionals who form the Encore family. "I have the best job in the world," he says, "which is essentially about making people happy." They aim to do this at Encore with genuinely warm service, a vibrant yet relaxed setting, and of course, the quality of the food.

The highly contemporary menu at Encore isn't weighed down with any 'boring staples' but instead takes diners to new heights by breaking the mould and embracing new values. This includes the small and big plate concept, which allows guests to eat tapas-style and share with friends as the dishes arrive in waves, or opt for a more traditional structure with a starter followed by a main course. Head chef Jordan Oates uses

locally sourced seasonal ingredients to build dishes around, and most things are freshly made on site, down to house kimchi, a range of breads (from the restaurant's sourdough starter, affectionately named Bill) and elegant desserts. The menus also include a glossary of 'fancy' culinary terms so everyone can order with confidence.

Encore is unique for the area and actively strives to make its offering different from the rest. It's not trying to be a fine dining establishment, because Gareth wants customers to relax and feel at home. Wellbeing plants help to create a warm and welcoming atmosphere. The cork mosaic, living wall and upcycled sound baffles all help to improve the acoustics of the space for the diner's extra comfort. "I want guests to feel like they can enjoy expertly crafted dishes in a relaxed setting." Food, service and ambience are all attended to with careful attention to detail, and the team's love of great hospitality infuses Encore with that special something to draw people back time and again.

HAGGIS RISOTTO, CRISPY KALE, HEN'S EGG, MUSTARD

As you would expect, quality ingredients are the key to creating an exceptional dish. The haggis used in this recipe is the award-winning Lancashire haggis from our local family butchers, Browns the Butchers of Chorley. We use our red wine jus made from veal bones for this recipe, but a good quality beef stock will do the trick.

5g Dijon mustard

5g English mustard

5g wholegrain mustard

50ml white wine vinegar

2 medium hen's eggs

100g kale, washed and picked

Pinch of salt

FOR THE RISOTTO

1 large shallot, finely sliced

100g Arborio (risotto) rice

25ml white wine

200ml good quality/homemade beef stock

40g Browns Lancashire haggis

25g unsalted butter

10g Parmesan, grated

15g parsley, finely chopped

Handful of pea shoots, to garnish

Start by drying out the mustard on a tray at the very bottom of an oven preheated to 180°c for 2 to 3 hours, then cool and blitz together into powder form.

Boil a pan of water with a generous splash of white wine vinegar in, then turn down to a simmer and gently crack the eggs into the water and cook for 3 and a half minutes. Remove and place in ice cold water. If you don't have a fryer, heat some oil in a pan and place the washed and picked kale into the hot oil for roughly 1 minute. Remove and drain the crispy leaves then season with salt.

FOR THE RISOTTO

Start by cooking the shallot in a large pan. Once it has cooked through, add the rice and stir constantly. When the rice starts to brown slightly add all of the white wine and cook on a medium heat until all the liquid has been absorbed. Slowly add the beef stock, roughly 50ml at a time, until it has all been absorbed and the rice only has a slight crunch.

Next add the haggis and butter, continue to cook over a medium heat for 2 to 3 minutes, then stir in the Parmesan and parsley. Remove the risotto from the heat and let it sit while you drop the poached eggs back into boiled water for 1 minute to reheat them.

TO SERVE

Spoon the risotto into serving bowls, top with some crispy kale and a poached egg, sprinkle the egg with mustard powder and garnish with pea shoots.

Preparation time: 2 hours | Cooking time: 20 minutes | Serves: 2

GROUNDED IN

GREAT COFFEE

EXCHANGE COFFEE COMPANY'S ETHOS CENTRES AROUND THE DAILY ROASTING OF COFFEE, SUPPORTING LOCAL SUPPLIERS AND MAKING PEOPLE FEEL AT EASE WHEN IT COMES TO CHOOSING THEIR TEA AND COFFEE.

Exchange Coffee Company has been in business for over 30 years with three roasting shops, two coffee bars, and a wholesale roastery in an old Baptist chapel including a service repair centre and barista training school. Such an established footing is built on the coffee and tea merchant's endeavour to always buy the best beans and roast them fresh, so that the quality shines through in the tasting. The two main shops are based in Blackburn and Clitheroe. Here, customers can see the coffee being roasted and then choose from over 35 coffees and 70 teas.

Any of the coffees and teas can be sampled in the coffee houses with a bite to eat from the selection of fresh and homemade breakfast, lunch and afternoon tea options. In Blackburn, the original coffee house, roastery and shop are housed within the Exchange Arcade. The grand old building in Fleming Square has retained a sense of Victorian finery and makes an opulent change to the trend for contemporary industrial decor. The same goes for Clitheroe's three storey coffee house, both with their William Morris wallpaper and antique wooden furniture.

It's important to general manager Richard and the whole Exchange team that customers can come into one of their shops and get personal recommendations, stories behind the products, and an enjoyable experience. People can buy online too of course from anywhere in the UK, and the wholesale aspect of the company supplies to many businesses throughout Lancashire as well as neighbouring counties. Despite links to numerous international destinations through the coffee and tea, Exchange is firmly rooted in the area and uses local produce wherever possible for the food, snacks, sweet treats and gifts.

Recently opportunities have arisen to buy from smaller cooperatives in countries that haven't previously been known as coffee producers, that work with women who are making inroads into the coffee industry where before they were excluded. Rainforest Alliance certified beans form a significant part of the company's product range, one of which, Brazil Ipanema Yellow Bourbon, garnered a two star gold Great Taste award in 2018 and was also used in collaboration with Lancashire producer Choc Amor to create a coffee chocolate bar. These kinds of partnerships have resulted in some fantastic products for Exchange and helps flourishing markets develop, showing a commitment on both sides to improving the quality of coffee available all over the world, but especially in Lancashire!

GREAT COFFEE
WITH A MOKA POT

You may not be a trained barista, but with a little attention to detail you can brew amazing espresso-style coffee in one of these inexpensive little Italian gadgets and also create foaming milk without having to invest in an expensive espresso machine! We always encourage experimenting for personal preferences. Have fun!

EQUIPMENT

Moka pot

French press

Freshly roasted coffee

Your choice of milk (full fat, skimmed, soya, oat, almond etc.)

Barista milk-frothing jug (optional)

Kettle

Saucepan

Your favourite cup

Boil the kettle and grind your coffee. It needs to be slightly coarser than espresso but slightly finer than filter. After letting the water cool for a few minutes, fill the bottom of your moka pot to just below the safety valve.

Insert the funnel of your moka pot into the brewer bottom. Fill with the ground coffee but do not push the coffee down, just leave it slightly heaped. Using a tea towel (be careful, it will be hot!) screw it together nice and tightly so the seal is complete.

Place the moka pot on a stove over a medium to high heat. Leave the top lid open. The coffee will begin to come out. As soon as you hear a gurgling noise, close the lid, switch off the heat and run the bottom of the pot underneath a cold tap to stop the brewing process. This is to stop the coffee developing a metallic taste. The idea is to get a relatively small amount of coffee which is rich and concentrated.

Set the moka pot aside and heat up some milk in a saucepan, being very careful not to boil it. Pour the milk into your French press and pump the plunger up and down vigorously until the milk significantly increases in volume.

Pour the coffee from your moka pot into your pre-warmed cup. You can then either transfer the milk to a barista jug or pour from the French press itself. Pour out the side of the jug for a cappuccino or from the spout for a latte or flat white. You can vary the amount of milk you use to replicate different drinks. If you prefer an Americano, simply top up your coffee with some hot water from the kettle. Enjoy your coffee!

A TASTE OF

SUNNY SPAIN

FINO TAPAS BRINGS A GENEROUS HELPING OF AUTHENTIC SPANISH FOOD AND DRINK TO PRESTON, BRIGHTENING UP EVEN THE GREYEST DAY WITH MEDITERRANEAN FLAVOURS AMIDST A COLOURFUL SETTING.

As with his first venture, the burger bar We Don't Give A Fork, Mark O'Rourke gave the restaurant that is now Fino Tapas a complete makeover when he bought it. The venue was done out with a modern Mediterranean look which instantly transports customers to sunny Spain in preparation for the feast of authentic food and drink that awaits them. Mark loves the culture around eating out in Spain – whiling the day away with a beer and an endless supply of delicious dishes to nibble on – and since there were no tapas restaurants in Preston at the time, he decided to create one.

That was in June 2018, and the team have recently designed a redeveloped menu to celebrate Fino's one year birthday. Many dishes are typically Andalusian and Catalonian, and to keep things as true to the original as possible many ingredients and drinks are imported from Spain. The restaurant has a wood-fired oven for steaks and whole fish, which are sourced locally to use the best Lancashire produce. With this in mind, inspiration comes from what's in season, such as courgette flowers – deep fried and stuffed with goat's cheese – that are only available for about ten weeks of the year. The greengrocers also bring a box of fruit and veg in every month for the chefs to create new dishes with, marrying Spanish flavour with freshly grown goodness. Even the oven was handmade in Spain and brought over!

Mark has previously worked with many of the chefs now at Fino, so they share an understanding of top quality food and have the depth of knowledge to deliver it. The unpretentious atmosphere might seem at odds with high end food, but it's all part of the dining experience Mark aims to create. Spanish music and décor enhance the feeling of a relaxed Mediterranean afternoon or evening, featuring colourful handmade tiles and photography that Mark has collected. From his first job in a tapas restaurant to the popular Preston destination he has created, Mark's love of Spanish food and culture shines through at Fino and helps to make the tapas experience a truly authentic one.

MODERN TAPAS SELECTION

*Barbecued sardines, potatoes with a spicy tomato sauce, and hot garlicky prawns
are Spanish staples. At the restaurant we use a wood-fired oven to recreate the
smoky barbecue effect, but a griddle pan will work so you can enjoy this mouth-
watering tapas all year round.*

FOR THE SARDINAS

1kg fresh sardines
2 cloves of garlic, sliced
1 tbsp smoked paprika
1 lemon, zested and juiced
4 tbsp olive oil
Pinch of sea salt

FOR THE PATATAS BRAVAS

2 tbsp olive oil
1 onion, finely chopped
3 cloves of garlic, crushed
1 small fairly hot red chilli, finely chopped
400g tin of chopped tomatoes
1 tbsp smoked paprika
Pinch of sugar
500g new potatoes, halved (leave the skins on)
Oil for deep frying
60g mayonnaise
½ tsp black pepper
2 cloves of garlic, crushed
Small bunch of chives, finely chopped

FOR THE GAMBAS PIL PIL

80ml olive oil
24 king prawns
2 tsp dried chili flakes
2 tsp smoked paprika
4 cloves of garlic, sliced
Small bunch of parsley, finely chopped

FOR THE SARDINAS

Remove the head and tail of the sardines if you like, then marinate the fish overnight in the garlic, paprika, lemon zest and olive oil.

Prepare the barbecue or heat a griddle pan until very hot. Cook the sardines for 3 or 4 minutes on each side until really caramelised, then sprinkle with salt to taste and squeeze over the juice of a lemon (reserving one teaspoon for the patatas bravas) before serving as they are.

FOR THE PATATAS BRAVAS

First make the sauce. Heat the oil in a saucepan over a low to medium heat. Add the onion and sweat until softened and translucent, about 10 minutes. Add the garlic and chilli and cook, stirring, for 1 minute. Now add the tomatoes, paprika, sugar and some salt and pepper. Simmer for about 10 minutes.

Meanwhile, deep fry the potatoes until they are nice and crispy. Drain on kitchen towel to remove excess oil.

Mix the mayonnaise with the black pepper, crushed garlic and the reserved teaspoon of lemon juice for an easy aioli.

To serve, put the deep fried potatoes in a bowl, smother them in tomato sauce, add a big dollop of aioli on top, and then finish with some chopped chives.

FOR THE GAMBAS PIL PIL

Heat the olive oil in a large pan. When the oil is hot, add the prawns and cook for about 2 minutes, stirring constantly. Add the chilli flakes, paprika, garlic and chopped parsley then stir well. Cook for 1 more minute, then season with salt and serve straightaway. The prawns need to be sizzling hot!

For the sardinas: Preparation time: 5 minutes, plus overnight | Cooking time: approx. 5 minutes | Serves: 4-6
For the patatas bravas: Preparation time: 30 minutes | Cooking time: 15 minutes | Serves: 4-6
For the gambas pil pil: Preparation time: 10 minutes | Cooking time: 5 minutes | Serves: 4-6

NOT JUST

PUB GRUB

FREEMASONS AT WISWELL IS A RENOWNED DESTINATION FOR SOPHISTICATED FOOD IN A RELAXED SETTING, HEADED UP BY LOCAL CHEF STEVEN SMITH.

The journey began in 2009 when chef owner Steven Smith took on Freemasons at Wiswell with the aim of creating a world-class foodie destination in a pub environment. Nestled in the beautiful countryside of Ribble Valley, the unique venture combines country pub with a twist of contemporary creativity and flair to create the perfect setting for a memorable gastronomic experience.

The ambience will soon work its magic and draw you into its relaxed charm. Front-of-house staff are friendly, professional and care most about your enjoyment. In the kitchen, Steven's team is dedicated to achieving impressive and consistent results using the finest seasonal ingredients available. His mission statement is to provide the ultimate gastronomic experience in a stylish pub setting that feels as relaxed as your own front room. The inventive menus feature indulgent dishes for lunch, early supper, à la carte dining and a three course Sunday lunch to suit all tastes. Private dining is also very well catered for in four different upstairs rooms, and 'Mr Smith's' will soon offer an exclusive experience for tables of 10, or four just off of the kitchen itself.

Steven was born in nearby Blackburn and learned his craft in some of the north's top establishments before going solo in the quaint medieval Lancashire village of Wiswell. His efforts haven't gone unnoticed, as Freemasons has recently proved its staying power by retaining its status as the country's best pub in the Waitrose Good Food Guide for three years running, AA Restaurant of the Year for England, number three in the Top 50 Gastropubs and Great British Pubs Best Food Pub, as well as Steven taking home the Top 50 Gastropubs Chef of the Year and Great British Pubs Chef of the Year.

Steven's aim going forward is to continually improve the offering for his loyal diners and push the boundaries of modern pub food, making the Freemasons synonymous with excellence for both cooking and service. He and the team now enjoy welcoming diners from far and wide, who have travelled specifically to dine there. The plan is always to continue to evolve and grow, which will soon take the form of a brand new kitchen and bedrooms which are being added to provide accommodation for those guests travelling specially to eat at the pub, proving its reputation precedes it and that Steven will continue to make his mark on the culinary landscape in Lancashire's countryside.

DUCK BREAST WITH LAVENDER, FENNEL AND PEACH

We're big fans of game at Freemasons and duck is a truly fantastic ingredient to work with and create recipes for. The richness of the meat is offset by the other flavours and it's a really attractive dish to plate up; great for impressing guests!

6 peaches

15ml white balsamic vinegar

100g honey

10g lavender

200ml orange juice

2 litres chicken stock

600g duck breast, on the bone

Olive oil

Salt

2 fennel bulbs

4 baby fennel

Chives, to garnish

Begin by preparing the compressed peach. Halve one of the peaches and remove the stone, then carefully peel off the skin. Place the flesh into a vacuum pack bag with a small dash (about 5ml) of balsamic vinegar. Seal the bag tightly and leave in the fridge to marinate for 1 to 2 hours (depending on how much time you have.)

Heat the honey in a pan until bubbling and caramelised, then add the lavender and orange juice. Reduce the sauce on a high heat for 3 minutes, then simmer and cook for 5 minutes. Add the chicken stock, stir and then simmer for 1 hour, or until it has reduced to a sauce-like consistency. Pass through a fine sieve and then set aside until ready to plate.

30 minutes before cooking, remove the duck from the fridge and allow it to reach room temperature, then preheat the oven to 160°c. Gently rub the duck breasts with olive oil, season and place on a baking tray. Roast in the oven for 40 minutes.

Meanwhile, prepare the purées. For the fennel purée, thinly slice the fennel bulbs including the tips and leaves. Place a shallow pan on a medium heat and add a small dash of oil. Sweat the fennel until soft, then add 100ml of water and cook until soft. Tip the mix into a blender, blitz until smooth then season to taste. Pass through a fine strainer and set aside until ready to serve.

For the peach purée, cook the remaining five peaches in simmering water for 15 minutes. Drain, halve and remove the stones. Purée the flesh and skins in a blender until smooth, then add the remaining vinegar (about 10ml) and purée again. Pass through a fine strainer and set aside.

Cut each baby fennel into quarters and cook in salted simmering water for 10 to 15 minutes. Strain and then sear in a hot pan with a dash of oil until browned on both sides. Remove from the pan and keep warm. Meanwhile, remove the compressed peaches from the fridge and allow them to reach room temperature. Rest the duck out of the oven for 10 minutes before carving into rectangular pieces (or as preferred).

Roll the duck in the honey and lavender sauce. Plate the dish with elegant spoonfuls of the fennel purée, dots of peach purée, baby fennel and compressed peach. Garnish with chopped chives and fennel fronds and serve immediately. Enjoy!

Preparation time: 2 hours | Cooking time: 1 hour | Serves: 2

GOOD OLD
PUB GRUB WITH A VIEW

HOMEMADE FOOD IS AT THE HEART OF THIS COUNTRY PUB WITH A CONTEMPORARY FEEL, THANKS TO A MOUTH-WATERING MENU OF PIES, PIZZAS AND MORE.

The Green Man at Inglewhite is a country pub with a difference, situated on the village green at the foot of Beacon Fell. It has been serving locals for many years, and came under new management in May 2016, leading to the pub becoming a Freehouse in April 2019 complete with a brand new selection of beers and wines. Previously, the old building was managed by chains and suffered mixed fortunes, but owner Mick O'Hara who runs Mikoh Inns Ltd bought The Green Man with a view to providing a relaxing environment for customers to enjoy good homemade food in, with a big emphasis on being family friendly.

Whether they are regulars, walkers with muddy boots, cyclists, weekend visitors driving out to enjoy the countryside or four-legged friends, everyone is welcomed like an old friend when they arrive at The Green Man. Great service is important in creating the warm atmosphere that characterises a great pub, alongside tasty food of course. Everything on the menu is freshly made by the chefs, from 'classic pub grub' to pizza.

The pub is best known for hearty pies with handcut chips which include a seasonal special, perfect for a cosy meal in front of an open fire (there are three to choose from) with a real ale or glass of wine to sip at your side.

For sunnier months there are tables out the front and a large beer garden at the back, boasting countryside views all round and plenty of space for children to play while adults relax on comfy outdoor seating. The Green Man's own camping field adjoins the beer garden and has pitches for tents and caravans so holidaymakers can stay and enjoy the scenery. A calendar of regular events provides fun for everyone over the summer, including a monthly quiz, darts teams, bank holiday barbecues, wine tasting sessions and a beer festival.

From light lunches to weekend treats, The Green Man offers a spot of proper Lancashire nourishment in a beautiful rural setting. The team aim to make it the perfect place to pop by with the whole family, and you might even get a friendly hello from the pub dog Benny too.

PORK, PICKLE & CHEESE
SHORTCRUST PASTRY PIE

This pork, pickle and cheese pie is a firm favourite on our menu. Encased in a rich buttery crust, the bold flavour combinations give you a scrumptious filling. It's humble pie with a little bit more depth!

FOR THE SHORTCRUST PASTRY

340g plain flour, sieved

½ tsp salt

225g butter, chilled and cubed, plus extra for greasing

1 large egg, beaten

3 tbsp cold water

FOR THE PIE FILLING

500g 5% fat pork mince

1 tsp tarragon

1 clove of garlic, finely diced

Salt and cracked black pepper

280g sweet pickle (small chunk variety)

100g mature cheese, grated

1 large egg, beaten

FOR THE SHORTCRUST PASTRY

Combine the sieved flour and salt in a large bowl. Add the cubes of butter and rub them into the flour using the tips of your fingers, letting it fall to aerate the mixture, until it looks like fine breadcrumbs. Add the beaten egg and one tablespoon of cold water. Stir the mixture with a round bladed knife and combine well before adding a further tablespoon of water.

Once the mixture starts to go lumpy, use your hand to combine the mixture. Try not to handle the dough too much. Add a tiny bit more water as you go if necessary, and don't worry if you think it's too dry at this stage. The dough should come together in a ball the more you mix it, and the bowl should be completely cleaned (i.e. not sticky). The dough should be dry enough to not stick to your hands, and quite stiff. Once the pastry is ready, place it in the fridge to rest for 20 minutes.

Preheat the oven to 180°c. Grease a 24cm pie dish with butter, then on a lightly floured surface, roll out a third of the chilled pastry for the pie lid, using the dish as a guide and making it a little larger, then chill again. Roll out the remaining pastry and line the dish with it. Make a few pinpricks in the bottom with a fork. Chill the pastry base, covered with cling film, for 15 minutes, and then bake in the preheated oven for 5 minutes, covering just the bottom with tin foil. Leave the oven on while you make the filling.

FOR THE PIE FILLING

Gently part cook the mince in a frying pan for a couple of minutes until it's no longer raw but still very tender. Add the tarragon and garlic, season with salt and pepper, then mix gently.

Transfer half the mince into the pastry case, then layer half the sweet pickle and half the cheese on top. Repeat this process to fill the pie. Top with the chilled pastry lid and seal the edges by pressing down all around with the back of a fork. Brush the top with the beaten egg to glaze all the exposed pastry. Bake the pie for 35 minutes or until the pastry is golden and the filling is piping hot, then serve immediately.

Preparation time: 20 minutes | Cooking time: 45 minutes | Serves: 4 (hearty portions)

JOURNEYS OF DISCOVERY

BOWLAND FOOD HALL IS ALL ABOUT SHOWCASING THE BEST OF LANCASHIRE'S FOOD AND DRINK PRODUCERS IN AN EXCITING AND CONTEMPORARY SETTING, WHICH INCLUDES A BUSTLING CAFÉ, TASTING TABLES AND MUCH MORE.

In the market town of Clitheroe, at the gateway to the Ribble Valley and the Forest of Bowland, the Holmes Mill complex is an epicurean heaven with Bowland Food Hall at its heart. This vast and industrial yet warm and welcoming space is a platform for producers to showcase their culinary creations. Most of these are small independent artisans who farm or grow within the county, keeping food miles down, and much of the meat and dairy is sourced within the surrounding Area of Outstanding Natural Beauty, but if it can't be found close to home, the best will be searched out further afield.

The proud but not parochial approach to finding top notch produce is down to Alison Ashworth, the 'BFF' or Bowland Food Finder of the venue. She goes out to discover new producers throughout the year, and eagerly welcomes even very seasonal goods, such as small scale local honey, to the line-up. These stay on the shelves for as long as they're available, alongside those who sell their goods all year round without having to rely solely on occasional markets and events.

Bowland Brewery, Butlers Farmhouse Cheeses, Bowland Forest Eggs and Cowman's Famous Sausage Shop are just a few of the Lancashire gems represented in the food hall, and their local delicacies and specialities are also used in the café which sits amidst the Aladdin's cave of produce. Grab a snack while shopping, sit down for a light lunch, indulge with a piece of freshly baked cake and a hot drink, or enjoy nibbles with your favourite tipple: the menu has something for everyone at any time of day, and if you stumble across a new favourite cheese or jam, chances are you can pick some up to take home afterwards!

The friendly and enthusiastic team within the Food Hall genuinely enjoy discussing their products with shoppers and visitors, creating a shopping experience rather than a mere shopping trip. Callum and Joe, the Food Hall Butcher Boys, are passionate about their work, championing high-welfare and sustainable meats, developing their own rubs and marinades, and striving to deliver the perfect cut of meat every time. When it comes to passion, enthusiasm and in-depth knowledge about Lancashire's fabulous food and drink there's no better place to celebrate the bounty of the county!

SOMETHING'S
BREWING

HOLMES MILL IS AN AMBITIOUS EPICUREAN DESTINATION BOASTING A FOOD HALL, BEER HALL, BISTRO, BAR AND GRILL, LUXURY HOTEL AND MORE.

The wonders inside an old textiles mill in the heart of Clitheroe are not something you'd expect to find outside of a city, but such is the pride in the food and hospitality of Lancashire, Holmes Mill exists just to celebrate it. The three sections of the Industrial Revolution-era building house complementary but individual parts of the whole, and the New Mill is where you'll find the Beer Hall and the brewery it showcases. In 2018 the venue won CAMRA's Best Pub Conversion, and was the only winner outside of London: another reason to be proudly Lancastrian!

Bowland Brewery's flagship tasting parlour is an ale enthusiast's paradise on a truly impressive scale. A minimum of 24 individual cask beers plus 42 hand pulls can be found behind one of the longest bars in the country at 105 feet, and that's on top of the bespoke kegs, bottled beers and cans also on offer. Like the Bowland Food Hall in the Weaving Shed next door, industrial décor and design mingles with a warm ambience that can be enjoyed in individual rooms or at Bavarian-style communal tables. Regular events like free music sessions, comedy, meet the brewer evenings and tastings also take place alongside 'New Beer Thursday' which introduces 24 beers to the line-up every week.

Drinking and dining co-exist happily in the beer hall, with a menu that covers nibbles to proper 'tucker' and can be paired perfectly with a beer. If more upmarket dining is your preference, the 1823 Spinning Block Bistro, Bar and Grill comprises a modern British steak and seafood restaurant just next door. With access to the best ingredients via Bowland Food Hall, the chefs transform the finest produce into stunning dishes that feature meats from Bowland and Lancashire, seafood from Fleetwod, Lancashire and the Manchester markets, fruit and vegetables from the West Lancashire growing country and other local delights.

The Bistro, Bar and Grill is the latest addition to Holmes Mill but won't be the last; plans are already in place to open a four screen Everyman cinema by the end of 2019. The problem of too much to see, do and eat in one day is handily resolved by the boutique 39 bedroom hotel in the Spinning Block, which provides a great base to explore not only Holmes Mill but Clitheroe and the county that offers up such a glorious array of food and drink to be celebrated there.

BOWLAND FOOD HALL
LANCASHIRE SHARING BOARD

What could be simpler than creating your very own Bowland Food Hall Sharing Board? With a few minutes preparation and the time it takes to wander around our artisan market you can recreate one of our most popular dishes. Make use of some of Lancashire's premier food producers to create a dish perfect for a lazy afternoon with a good bottle of wine or one of Bowland's beautiful ales.

1 Holmes-made Lancashire Cheese and Red Onion Marmalade Quiche

100g Greenfields Crumbly Lancashire Cheese

1 packet of Stocktons Oatcakes

1 jar of Tracklements Apple Cider and Brandy Chutney

1 Famous Roy Porters Pork Pie

1 jar of Heritage Kitchen Piccalilli

1 bag of Lancashire Salted Crisps

Dressed salad leaves, to garnish

Pop the quiche in the oven and warm gently at around 150°c for around 10 minutes. Next, slice the cheese thinly – don't worry too much about it crumbling – and lay the flakes of cheese over an oatcake, then pop a generous spoonful of chutney over the top.

Cut the pork pie in half and arrange on the board, adding as much piccalilli as you want.

Once the quiche is warm, transfer it to the board and garnish with some dressed salad.

Serve the Lancashire Sharing Board with a chilled Sauvignon Blanc or a pint of Bowland Hen Harrier: both work just as well. Alternatively, pop into Bowland Food Hall and you can let us take care of it while you relax and enjoy the surroundings!

Preparation time: 10 minutes | Serves: 2 (or one very hungry person!)

COQ AU VIN JAUNE
(CHICKEN IN WHITE WINE SAUCE)

A great French classic, served with smooth buttery mashed potato and fine green beans. When buying your chicken, make sure you ask the butcher nicely to take out the thigh bone and French trim the top of the legs.

FOR THE CHICKEN

2 Portobello mushrooms, sliced

4 chicken legs, French trimmed (the food hall butchery counter can to do this for you)

4 rashers of pancetta

1 large onion, roughly diced

1 carrot, roughly diced

3 sticks of celery, roughly diced

5 cloves of garlic, minced

4 sprigs of thyme

200ml white wine

1 litre brown chicken stock (use homemade if you can)

FOR THE MASH

4 large Maris Piper potatoes

200ml milk

200g unsalted butter, cubed

FOR THE SAUCE

4 Portobello mushrooms, sliced

200g shallots, finely diced

4 sticks of celery, finely diced

400ml Madeira

150ml double cream

1 small packet of flat leaf parsley, picked and chopped

TO SERVE

Green beans, steamed and buttered

FOR THE CHICKEN

Fry the sliced mushrooms, seasoned with salt and pepper, in a little oil until softened slightly. Drain and leave to cool, then stuff the mushrooms into the cavity left by the thigh bone in the chicken legs. Shape the meat to conceal the mushrooms then wrap the whole leg tightly in a slice of pancetta.

In a large pan on a high heat, seal the chicken thighs thoroughly using tongs to turn. Set aside.

Put the onion, carrot, celery, garlic and thyme into the same pan used to seal the chicken. Fry until the onion starts to soften, de-glaze the pan with the white wine then add the chicken back in. Pour over the stock and cover, then simmer very gently (just a bubble every few seconds) for 45 minutes to an hour, or until the meat is tender. Transfer the chicken to a tray and place in the oven on a low heat to keep warm. Pass the liquid through a fine sieve into a jug.

FOR THE MASH

Thoroughly wash the potatoes and place them, unpeeled, in a pan of cold water with a little salt. Bring to the boil and simmer gently until you can slide a knife in with no resistance. Drain and leave to steam dry. Gently peel off the skin, then put the potato through a ricer back into the pan. Warm the milk with a splash of water in a clean pan. Meanwhile, heat the potatoes for around 5 minutes, stirring gently, to dry them over a low heat. Slowly add the butter and stir quickly to give the mash a creamy consistency. Add the warm milk and whip energetically to make it smooth. Taste and season well.

FOR THE SAUCE

Sauté the mushrooms in a little oil quickly, then remove the mushrooms and sauté the shallots and celery. Add the Madeira, reduce by 80%, add the sieved liquid and bring to the boil. Reduce until the sauce thickens slightly, then add the cream and reduce until it coats the back of a spoon. Drop the chicken and mushrooms back in and baste with the sauce. Stir through the chopped parsley to finish.

TO SERVE

Spoon the mash into a bowl and make a little well in the centre. Gently place the chicken on top and spoon the sauce over the leg, flooding the well. Serve with buttered green beans.

Preparation time: 45 minutes | Cooking time: 2-3 hours | Serves: 4

A BED AND BREAKFAST

LIKE NO OTHER

LANCASTER BARN B&B IS MORE THAN ROOMS AND BREAKFAST: THESE ARE
THE FOUNDATIONS THAT OWNERS CLARE AND PAUL HAVE BUILT ON TO
PROVIDE A UNIQUE AND INDIVIDUAL EXPERIENCE FOR EVERY GUEST.

Clare and Paul had plenty of experience running pubs and restaurants, but were looking for something smaller and more personal to create themselves. When a farmhouse with a disused barn came up for sale they knew it was a great opportunity to turn their vision into a reality, so after completely renovating the buildings the couple threw an opening party for the local community in late 2018. Within just a few months Lancaster Barn B&B had taken bookings for the following summer as well as events and wedding parties far in advance. Its runaway success so far is a testament to how much Clare and Paul have elevated the concept of a B&B at their bespoke and beautifully designed venue.

The nine double rooms all have ensuites and design features that are intended to make each one a relaxed and calming space, such as natural linen and wool carpets against oak furniture and light stone interiors. "We wanted it to feel contemporary but really comfortable," says Clare. The big breakfast room follows this trend, with glass on three sides letting in the sunshine and views of Lancashire farmland to start a great day with. Focusing on the most important meal of any day, Lancaster Barn serves a mixture of traditional and healthier options including a veggie breakfast that's nearly as popular as the full English! Organic bread, free-range eggs and other local produce forms the basis of every freshly made dish, and the food is complemented by tea and coffee from Atkinsons, a merchant that has been based in Lancashire since the early 1800s.

Combining old and new is something Clare and Paul have embraced within their venture, and during the restoration energy-saving measures were introduced to make the old barn as eco-friendly as possible. This ethos extends to organic toiletries, the elimination of single-use plastics, and plans to build cycle storage with the possibility of bikes available to hire for guests in the near future. There's plenty to see and do nearby, including evening meals at the B&B's nearest neighbour and foodie destination, The Bay Horse Inn, which has a lovely intertwined history with Lancaster Barn as well as a strong connection today so guests can enjoy the best of both venues.

From the little details carefully selected by Clare and Paul that make all the difference, to the roots Lancaster Barn has in the community and the land around it, a stay there promises to leave you rejuvenated and ready for a return visit!

EARL GREY OATS

A super-charged bowl of goodness which is also vegan and dairy-free: what's not to love? Infusing the almond milk with Earl Grey tea adds a subtle scent, elevating the humble oats to a level of sophistication, which are then loaded with blueberries and nuts, drizzled with homemade almond maple butter and sprinkled with crunchy chia seeds and 100% cacao chocolate for a superfood indulgence!

FOR THE OATS

800ml unsweetened almond milk

4 tsp Earl Grey tea (we use Atkinsons loose leaf)

4 tsp organic agave nectar

160g oats

FOR THE ALMOND MAPLE BUTTER

150g almonds

20ml maple syrup

Pinch of sea salt flakes

TO SERVE

50g whole almonds and hazelnuts, roughly chopped

1 punnet of blueberries

2 tsp chia seeds

100% cacao chocolate, chopped into small pieces

FOR THE OATS

Warm the almond milk in a saucepan over a medium heat then add the Earl Grey tea leaves. Remove from the heat and allow to infuse for 3 minutes. Strain the milk and sweeten to taste with the agave nectar. Return the infused milk back into the pan and add the oats. Cook over a medium heat, stirring occasionally, until the mixture is the desired consistency.

FOR THE ALMOND MAPLE BUTTER

Mix the almonds and maple syrup together in a bowl so the nuts are coated with the syrup. Spread the mixture onto a baking tray and roast in the oven at 190°c for 5 to 8 minutes. Allow to cool. Tip into a food processor, add a pinch of sea salt, and blend until creamy. The remaining almond butter will keep well in a sealed container.

TO SERVE

Spoon the oats into four serving bowls and top with the chopped nuts and blueberries. Drizzle with maple almond butter and sprinkle with chia seeds and chocolate. Serve immediately.

Preparation time: 10 minutes | Cooking time: 5 minutes | Serves 4

THE FIGHT FOR

FAIRER FOOD

EDUCATING PEOPLE – IN A WAY THAT ALLOWS THEM TO LEARN ABOUT AND ENJOY GOOD FOOD – ON THE IMPORTANCE OF CREATING BETTER SYSTEMS FOR FOOD FAIRNESS IS WHAT THE LARDER EXISTS TO DO.

The Larder is a social enterprise working towards 'food fairness for all' with Lancashire's farms, communities and small producers. Founder Kay set the project up after writing a sustainable food charter for the county, as a result of a series of food-related consultations. The idea of a food hub for learning about, cooking and eating good food came up during her work in Preston. Kay began on a voluntary basis, and after building an important space in the community she was awarded lottery funding to realise her vision.

Best described as a dietary education resource, today The Larder works in three main areas: experience, education and access. The café and catering business brings people in, providing a relaxed and informal environment in which customers can start to think about food differently. The food academy runs a range of basic to bespoke courses, workshops, training and masterclasses on everything from cookery to getting into college. Enabling access through outreach programmes and using food as a route into employment is another important part of the whole in the drive to create a better food system in the long term, which benefits not just farmers and consumers but animals, the environment and the planet.

Having grown up on a small farm in Lancashire and worked as a nutritionist, food and health have always been important to Kay, and she cites education as a fundamental element of The Larder. Along with her team, one of her main aims is to make it easier for businesses to buy locally and ethically when it comes to sourcing produce. Part of the project is about developing a mechanism to achieve this, and the café of course leads by example, setting fair prices for everybody involved and diverting money back into the enterprise rather than profit alone.

Suppliers are a crucial link in the chain The Larder is building, which is why they are all showcased at the café where customers can read about them and start to develop a better understanding of where produce comes from and why it's important to be aware of that provenance. A seasonally adaptable menu means little waste, and relies on strong relationships to make the most of fresh, locally grown ingredients. Joe's eggs, John's bread, Ian's organic meats, and the vegetable stall holder who buys directly from farmers make the journey from farm to fork that much shorter and more sustainable: this is what The Larder stands for and represents in its mission for food fairness.

LANCASHIRE RAREBIT

Proper comfort food, delicious any time of the day. We wanted to showcase the local producers that we work with, and what better way to do so than by partnering Dewlay Lancashire Tasty cheese with artisan sourdough made by John's Bread!

20g butter

20g flour

150ml milk

½ tsp wholegrain mustard

A dash of Lancashire sauce (or Worcestershire sauce)

Black pepper, to taste

60g Lancashire Tasty Cheese, grated

Salt, to taste

2 slices of sourdough bread

Dissolve the butter in a saucepan and add the flour. Stir until the mixture forms a smooth paste and sauté for a few minutes. Pour the milk slowly into the pan, stirring with a balloon whisk until the mixture blends together smoothly. Continue this process until all the milk has been added and then let it cook until the béchamel sauce thickens.

Add the mustard, Lancashire or Worcestershire sauce, black pepper and two thirds of the cheese to the pan. Reserve the remaining third of the cheese to sprinkle on top of the rarebit. Check the mixture in the pan for seasoning and add a little salt if necessary.

Divide the sauce over the two slices of sourdough, sprinkling the reserved cheese on top. Grill the rarebit under a medium heat for a few minutes, or until the sauce is golden and bubbling.

Serve up and tuck in!

Preparation time: 15 minutes | Cooking time: 20 minutes | Serves: 2

PUTTIN' ON

THE FITZ

NESTLED AMONGST THE PENNINES IN THE ROSSENDALE VALLEY SITS MR FITZPATRICK'S FACTORY, VINTAGE CORDIAL MAKERS DEDICATED TO REGENERATING A PIECE OF LANCASHIRE HISTORY.

Mr Fitzpatrick's began life in Dublin in 1836, when herbalist Julia Fitzpatrick created wonderful tonics, cordials and pick-me-ups for the locals. In 1899, the family moved to Northern England, establishing a successful chain of temperance bars. Unfortunately, after World War II interest in these declined and Mr Fitzpatrick's story was in danger of being lost forever. However, the current owners brought this piece of Lancashire history back to life in 2011; restored to its former glory, it's now the last remaining original temperance bar in Britain.

Although the company has moved on from its humble beginnings, the vintage-inspired cordials are still crafted in the same artisan tradition, made with natural ingredients and added botanical notes. All their drinks are vegan, gluten-free, and amazingly versatile. They can be used in an endless number of ways; serve straight up diluted with still, sparkling or tonic water, enjoy hot for a comforting treat, use in ices, delicious floats and milkshakes, as a splash mixer or cocktail base. You can even cook and bake with them. For lots of creative recipe and serving suggestions visit: www.mrfitzpatricks.com/recipe-home

The ideas never stop coming for the Mr Fitzpatrick's team, who create wonderful concoctions such as the universally liked Rhubarb & Rosehip or their latest Lemon, Yuzu and Turmeric cordial. The company has also found a niche with the Mr Fitz Aqua Spritz Systems, catering to the often forgotten non-drinkers who are demanding a better choice than the usual lacklustre offerings.

See them out and about at food and drink festivals across the country, buy online or in store at the many food halls, farm shops, garden centres and delis across the country, or try these delights at the very many watering holes; to find stockists visit: www.mrfitzpatricks.com/stockists

It's been an exciting journey of growth and development, but the company has stayed true to its botanical roots and dedication to artisan craftsmanship in creating these premium drinks. The innovative recipes acknowledge changing trends while resolutely adhering to the principles of their heritage. Through the team's passion and commitment, they continue to bring their wonderful drinks to a whole new generation of fans, keeping the Mr Fitzpatrick's legacy well and truly alive!

CRAFT GIN

SITUATED IN A RENOVATED MILL IN BURNLEY, LANCASHIRE'S FIRST DISTILLERY STAYS AHEAD OF THE GIN GAME WITH AN ETHOS OF HONESTY AND OPENNESS THAT SETS THEM APART FROM THE COMPETITION.

Inspired by his travels, director Phil enlisted nephew Ollie to help him in creating a unique line of spirits. After discovering a second basement in Ollie's house, Batch Gin was born. With everyone involved still working full time in the beginning, gin production was limited to evenings – with all wages paid in gin!

Being Lancashire's first distillery was an advantage, as it meant the team could take time in perfecting their recipe without pressure from competitors. Batch also went on to become the first single-distillery spirits subscription, allowing members to try and test flavours and give honest feedback that would shape the way future gins were crafted. Now head distiller Ollie is the brains behind the weird and wonderful recipes: a kind of mad scientist figure when it comes to unusual flavours and additions. Each bottle of Batch gin tells a unique story; from their Whinberry gin – named after a local berry that was hand-picked by Burnley natives in an annual competition – to the Big Trouble Gin, which is named after Ollie's dog Lo Pan, every gin is directly influenced by the team and their lives.

The shining star is their Industrial Strength Gin, a punchy Navy gin that nods to the industrial roots of their home town's heritage. This went on to win Double Gold and Best Gin medals at the 2018 San Francisco World Spirits Competition, meaning that the Lancashire born and bred spirit was judged as one of the best in the world, something that the team are extremely proud of. They have also gained local recognition as well as global, having been awarded Best Producer at the 2018 Lancashire Tourism Awards and Food and Drink Product of the Year for Lancashire Life in the same year.

However, the impressive string of awards they have under their belt hasn't made them lose sight of their roots. With the growing popularity of gin across the country, Batch makes sure to keep to their original ethos of honesty and openness to stay ahead of the game. They still only produce a small quantity of bottles, with each one still being signed by hand with the distiller's signature, giving them an authenticity through the team's commitment to care and attention to detail. As the team says with Tom Warner's hashtag #CraftisGraft, making proper craft gin is hard graft, but it's all about putting every inch of your heart and soul into each and every bottle.

THE GINGERBERRY

The pairing of ginger and lime with whinberries – a local Lancashire fruit that makes a gin similar to sloe but with its own unique flavour – is a lovely warming drink, and the fizzy rhubarb and rosehip concoction makes summer afternoons even sweeter. Batch's award-winning gins and Mr Fitzpatrick's beautiful botanical drinks are simply a match made in heaven!

Preparation time: 5 minutes | Serves: 1

50ml Batch Whinberry Gin

Ice

25ml Mr Fitzpatrick's Ginger Cordial

Tonic/sparkling water

Lime wheels

Frozen mixed berries

Pour the Whinberry Gin over a generous amount of ice in a serving glass. Add 25ml Mr Fitzpatrick's Ginger Cordial then top up with a good tonic water or sparkling water. Garnish with a lime wheel and frozen mixed berries.

THE FIZZ-PATRICK'S

Preparation time: 5 minutes | Serves: 1

25ml Batch Industrial Strength Gin

25ml Fitzpatrick's Rhubarb and Rosehip Cordial

25ml lemon juice

1 bar spoonful (approx. 5ml) of sugar syrup (optional)

Prosecco

Fresh sage leaves

Stir the Industrial Strength Gin and Fitzpatrick's Cordial with the lemon juice. If you prefer a sweeter drink, add the sugar syrup at this stage. Top up with Prosecco and garnish with a fresh sage leaf.

THE

SAUCE
OF LIFE

A LOVE OF GOOD HONEST FOOD AND A FLAIR FOR RECREATING
AUTHENTIC RECIPES LED ONE COUPLE TO TURNING A FLEDGING IDEA
INTO A THRIVING BUSINESS.

The Nowt Poncy Food Company was established in 2016, but has been 30 years in the making for partners in life and business, Karen and Julian. The two met at Manchester Polytechnic in the 80s and enjoyed going out for dinner when their student finances allowed, but were not fans of the 'nouvelle cuisine' trend that left diners with a tiny 'poncy' plateful at disproportionate prices! Anything they particularly liked went on their menu for the 'Nowt Poncy Bistro' of their imaginings. It was just a bit of fun, but when the opportunity to start up a food business of their own presented itself years later, what else could they call it but The Nowt Poncy Food Company?

It all began when they decided to jar up Julian's homemade cooking sauces as Christmas presents one year, and they got such fantastic feedback that it seemed worth making more of them. They began at home but quickly outgrew their kitchen, moving next into rented space, then their local catering college department and finally into the company's very own premises. This has given them a lot more scope for product development, and a range of luxury pasta which they import from a family-run business in Italy has already been added to the offering.

Tomato and Basil was the first sauce to be officially designated 'nowt poncy' and is made with only six ingredients. Top quality Italian tinned tomatoes, Lancashire vegetables and fresh herbs are essential to the whole range which means they are all vegan friendly (with the exception of The Big Easy Creole which contains Worcester Sauce) and gluten-free with no additives or preservatives of course. Julian has picked up recipes over the years, such as a traditional curry sauce from the Punjab region of India, and a Creole sauce given to him by a friend who got it from a restaurant in New Orleans. Arrabbiata and Pizza sauces complete the current range, which are all "as versatile as your imagination" when it comes to cooking with them.

With plenty more ideas in the pipeline for The Nowt Poncy Food Company, Karen and Julian plan to support other artisan producers and hope to encourage other companies to think more about quality and health when it comes to food, as they do with genuine passion and a commitment to food that's definitely 'nowt poncy' but delicious in every way!

QUICK AND EASY PASTA BAKE

Pasta bake is a family favourite in our house, but it can take a while to make. We use a jar of our sauce which cuts down the ingredient list and prep, reducing the recipe time!

500g good quality mince

250g mushrooms, sliced reasonably thickly

300g pasta

A jar of Nowt Poncy® Tomato & Basil Sauce

(or Nowt Poncy® Arrabbiata Sauce if you want to spice it up a bit!)

FOR THE CHEESE SAUCE

600ml milk

40g butter

40g plain flour

200g extra mature cheddar cheese, grated

Preheat the oven to 200°c (or 180°c for fan). Using a non-stick pan, fry off the mince. Keep it moving so it doesn't burn, and break it up as it's cooking. Once browned, drain the mince in a colander (this helps to keep the fat content down and keeps an eye on calories). Return the mince to the pan and add the mushrooms. Fry until the mushrooms are cooked through, then transfer the mixture to a bowl.

Bring a pan of water to the boil and cook the pasta until it's almost done. Drain the pasta REALLY well. This allows the pasta to soak up liquid from the sauce when the bake is assembled, making it even more delicious!

Return the mince and mushrooms to the same pan they were cooked in, stir in the jar of sauce and mix everything thoroughly. Bring to the boil, then add the pasta and stir well to coat in sauce. Make sure the filling is heated through then transfer the mixture to the deep ovenproof pan or casserole.

FOR THE CHEESE SAUCE

Warm the milk in a microwave for around 3 minutes. Wipe out the non-stick pan and warm the butter in it on a low heat until melted. Add the flour and blend together well. Keep it moving for a couple of minutes over the heat. This helps to get rid of the floury taste. Add a little of the warmed milk and mix thoroughly until you have a lump-free paste, then repeat this process until all the milk is blended, but remember to add a little bit at a time.

Once all of the milk has been added, the sauce should be smooth and thick enough to coat the back of a spoon but still pourable. Take it off the heat and stir in 150g of the cheese, keeping 50g aside.

TO ASSEMBLE

Cover the mince, mushroom and pasta mixture with the cheese sauce. Sprinkle the rest of the grated cheese over the top. Place the pasta bake in the oven and cook for about 20 to 25 minutes. The smell is amazing when it's warming through; you'll barely be able to keep your hands off it! Make sure the pasta bake is piping hot throughout before serving.

Serve with a fresh salad; of course if you're feeling hungry a nice wedge of garlic bread goes well with it too and helps to mop up the sauce at the end!

Preparation time: 30 minutes | Cooking time: 20-25 minutes | Serves: 4

WET YOUR WHISTLE,

FILL YOUR BELLY

OTTER'S POCKET ALE HOUSE IS ABOUT GREAT FOOD AND GREAT DRINKS IN EQUAL MEASURE WITHIN A COSY 'MICRO GASTROPUB' SETTING.

Mark O'Rourke has a knack for spotting venues with real potential and bringing new gastronomic experiences to Preston. Following the openings of We Don't Give A Fork and Fino Tapas, the restaurant owner turned a failing eatery on Winckley Street into Otter's Pocket Ale House. The interiors were completely gutted to transform the space, exposing original fireplaces and adding glass shelving for the bottles of wine and beer. It's designed to feel like a gastropub in miniature, with wood panelled walls and a tiled bar serving real ales and proper pies.

For real ale enthusiasts, this is the place to be in Preston. A selection of six craft beers is always on offer alongside three cask ales which rotate as soon as they're emptied, so you're never short of something new to try. Otter's Pocket also has over 50 wines and a generous range of spirits from gin to whisky. There's no scrimping on choice or quality here, and the same ethos is applied to the food menu which features classic pies, filled to the rafters and sent out with extra gravy.

"We want people to get their money's worth here," says Mark.

To this end, all the pies are made in house and use local produce such as fish landed at Fleetwood. They can also be made gluten-free, plus the menu has vegetarian and vegan options. What goes into the menus and how they are put together is very important to Mark. His background in both cheffing and management, as well as a natural passion for food and a desire to improve Preston's food and drink scene, has given him insight from different angles of the industry which he uses to create great venues.

Pie and pints demand a cosy setting to enjoy them in, which is just what Otter's Pocket provides. The atmosphere is relaxed and casual, so you can pop in for a drink or sit down for your dinner. Ordering and paying is done at the bar, so the venture has a flexibility that makes it feel really chilled from afternoon through to evening.

PRESTON'S BUTTER PIE

Butter Pie is also known as Catholic pie or Friday pie, and is an age-old dish from around the Chorley and Preston area. For non-Lancastrians, it's a potato pie!

FOR THE PASTRY

225g plain flour
A pinch of salt
50g salted butter, at room temperature
50g lard, at room temperature
Ice cold water

FOR THE FILLING

3 large potatoes
1 huge onion or 2 regular ones
1 tbsp white pepper
150g salted butter

FOR THE PASTRY

Sift the flour and salt into a bowl then stir in the butter and lard. Use your fingertips to rub the fats gently into the dry ingredients until the mixture resembles fine crumbs, then drizzle in just enough ice cold water to bring the pastry together. Form it into a ball, pop into a plastic bag and leave in the fridge to rest for 1 hour.

FOR THE FILLING

Meanwhile, peel the potatoes and the onion then slice them to about the thickness of a pound coin. Parboil the potatoes until they are just soft but still holding their shape, about 10 minutes. Sauté the onions over a low heat with the white pepper and 50g of the butter until they are soft.

Roll out about two thirds of the pastry, line a pie dish, and trim the edges.

Drain the potatoes, let the steam leave the pan, then layer the potatoes, onions and flakes of the remaining butter into the lined pie dish. Season the filling with salt and white pepper, then cover with the last third of the pastry, rolled out to make a lid. Crimp or press the edges together to seal the pastry and prick a hole in the centre to let out steam.

Bake the pie at 180°c for about 30 minutes until golden. Serve immediately with mash, gravy and pickled red cabbage.

Preparation time: 20 minutes | Cooking time: 30 minutes | Serves: 4

A FAMILY AFFAIR WITH
GREAT GASTRONOMY

FAMILY-OWNED SINCE NOVEMBER 2016, THE PLOUGH IS A GASTROPUB-STYLE ESTABLISHMENT WITH LOTS TO OFFER WHEN IT COMES TO BEAUTIFULLY COOKED FRESH FOOD.

Chef Matthew, front of house manager Karina, and bar manager Steven have two things in common: family and a passion for good old-fashioned pub hospitality with a bit of a twist. "We try to offer something that you won't find elsewhere in this area, and more of a dining experience than your standard pub meal." Matthew and Karina are partners in life and in the business, while Matthew's dad Steven is new to the industry. When they spotted The Plough was up for sale, it was a great opportunity to own their first establishment and push themselves to be the best they could be.

Recently the venue has been treated to big refurbishments that have opened up the upstairs space for more diners, added a separate dining room for up to twenty people, and refreshed the historical building which has been a pub for more than two centuries now. Just within the town of Oswaldtwistle yet boasting countryside views, The Plough aims to create an exciting experience for every customer who visits, whether they're a seasoned local or a passing tourist. Something of a hidden gem, it offers relaxed casual dining in sumptuous booths overlooked by the new addition of a blossom tree, and private dining for celebratory occasions.

The menu features home-cooked fish and chips, steak and ale pies, local dishes such as game and other hearty favourites. This traditional fare sits alongside an à la carte menu with more elegant and refined options, plus weekly changing specials. Matthew and his team of two chefs – Luke and Ronan – actively try and provide something for everyone with their varied menus, and work as a close-knit team to produce the best quality food they can. With strong professional backgrounds, and from Michelin-starred kitchens in Matthew's case, they have brought passion and talent to the homely gastropub environment of The Plough.

Steven takes great pride in serving cocktails and a wide selection of gins, wines and cask ales. Matthew, Karina and Steven very much believe their team are essential in producing an experience for diners that exceeds their expectations; The Plough team are very much like an extended family. For a Lancashire welcome and good pub food with a difference, The Plough has put itself forward as a frontrunner amidst the county's array of countryside dining establishments.

PAN SEARED WOOD PIGEON

This recipe celebrates the humble wood pigeon: a flavoursome dish that combines the earthy flavour of pigeon with sweet brioche and the added depth of red wine jus.

FOR THE PURÉE

1 butternut squash
2 sprigs of rosemary
200g salted butter

FOR THE JUS

500ml best quality beef stock
285ml red wine
2 tbsp redcurrant jelly

FOR THE PIGEON

6 wood pigeon breasts, lightly seasoned
50g salted butter
200g pancetta
500g mixed wild mushrooms
1 loaf of brioche, sliced into 2.5cm slices
Pea shoots, to garnish

FOR THE PURÉE

Peel the butternut squash, remove the seeds and cut the flesh into 5cm cubes. Cook the squash in boiling water with the rosemary until soft, then drain off the water and remove the rosemary. Blend the squash with the butter until smooth.

FOR THE JUS

Bring the beef stock to the boil in a saucepan, then add the red wine and redcurrant jelly. Reduce the amount of liquid by a quarter then keep warm until serving.

FOR THE PIGEON

Heat up two pans, both with a touch of oil in, and place the pigeon breasts in one of the pans. Seal on both sides then add half of the butter. Cook for a further 2 minutes on each side (longer if you would like the meat more well done) then place on a tray to rest for 2 minutes.

Add the pancetta to the second pan and cook until golden brown, then add the wild mushrooms and the remaining butter to cook for 1 minute. Transfer the pancetta and mushroom mixture to a plate lined with kitchen roll to remove any excess liquid. Lastly, toast the brioche slices.

TO PLATE

Plate the butternut purée, then the toasted brioche, and top with the mushrooms and pancetta. Halve the pigeon breasts and place one on each plate, over the mushrooms, then drizzle with red wine jus and garnish with fresh pea shoots.

Preparation time: 10 minutes | Cooking time: 25 minutes | Serves: 6

SMOKE AND KIPPERS

TRADITIONAL METHODS, NATURAL ENGLISH OAK WOOD SMOKE, AND QUALITY LANCASHIRE PRODUCE ARE THE NOT-SO-SECRET INGREDIENTS AT THE PORT OF LANCASTER SMOKEHOUSE.

The Port of Lancaster Smokehouse was set up by John and Patricia and passed down to their son Michael, who runs the small family business today. It began as a hobby, with John using traditional methods of preserving local fish to create delicious smoked delicacies. 2019 is the company's 41st year and restaurants, hotels, pubs and even cruise liners up and down the country are supplied with quality natural smoked food – you name it, they supply it.

The smokehouse still uses traditional methods of preparing, smoking and curing edibles with smouldering English oak and a healthy dose of respect for the heritage it has carried into the contemporary world of food. From fish to cheese, red meat to game and poultry, the smokehouse tries to source all its products as locally as possible, though the best herring and mackerel are brought in from Scotland. In season, fish can be delivered straight from the neighbouring River Lune and game is shot within the Trough of Bowland not more than ten miles away.

The factory and shop are based at Glasson Dock, where customers can buy directly from the range of products and even have a peek at the processes through the window. Tours are available too, and for those further afield everything is available online through the website. Complementary products such as pickles, chutneys, sauces and a selection of wines are also sold by the smokehouse, and the wide choice of gift hampers makes choosing a present for food lovers very easy!

The range has won an array of Great Taste awards, and has developed from a few core products as the company has grown. It is still close-knit though, with most of the staff living locally in the small village. "Our aim is to continue working as traditionally as possible, with a strong commitment to quality and a wealth of experience to draw on. We believe that our vital ingredient is time: the shortest time from catch to our smokehouse means freshness, and the slow smoking which develops such rich flavours in the produce. Working this way for as long as possible is our goal because it's the best way to produce excellent, delicious, smoked food."

LANCASTER SMOKED MACKEREL
OAT FISHCAKES WITH CHIVE CRÈME FRAÎCHE

This recipe was created in the earliest smokehouse days, over 40 years ago. It's the go-to comfort dish and packed full of Omega 3. We use our award-winning lemon and parsley smoked mackerel, but any of the other varieties will work just as well.

FOR THE FISHCAKES

600g potatoes

Pinch of salt

Pinch of black pepper

3 tbsp horseradish

5 spring onions, finely chopped

1 tbsp freshly chopped parsley

500g lemon and parsley smoked mackerel, skin removed and flaked into pieces

3 tbsp plain flour, seasoned with salt and pepper

2 eggs, beaten

300g fresh wholemeal breadcrumbs

3 tbsp oats

½ lemon, juiced

Vegetable oil, for shallow frying

FOR THE CHIVE CRÈME FRAÎCHE

100g crème fraîche

½ lemon, zested

2 tbsp fresh chives, finely diced

TO SERVE

Leafy side salad (optional)

FOR THE FISHCAKES

Peel and wash the potatoes, then cut them into chunks. Place these in a saucepan, cover with water, add salt and then bring to the boil. Ensure the potatoes are cooked through before draining. Add the black pepper and horseradish to the potato then mash until smooth.

Stir the spring onions, chopped parsley, lemon juice and flaked mackerel into the mash then form the mixture into eight equally sized patties. Place the fishcakes in the fridge to chill for 20 to 30 minutes.

Place the seasoned flour in one bowl, the beaten eggs in another, then combine the breadcrumbs and oats in another separate bowl.

FOR THE CHIVE CRÈME FRAÎCHE

Mix the crème fraîche, lemon zest and chives together then season to taste. Set aside.

Remove the fishcakes from the fridge. One at a time, lightly dust with the flour, dip into the egg then cover with the breadcrumb and oat mixture.

Heat 1cm of oil in a large frying pan over a medium to low heat. Shallow fry the coated fishcakes for 3 to 4 minutes on each side until they are golden, crispy and heated throughout. Remove them from the pan and place on kitchen paper to drain off any excess oil.

Serve with the crème fraîche dip and a fresh leafy salad on the side.

Preparation time: 20 minutes | Cooking time: 20 minutes | Serves: 4

PROUD
PRESTON

PRESTON BID HAS PLAYED AN IMPORTANT PART IN PRESTON'S THRIVING FOOD AND DRINK SCENE, AND IS COMMITTED TO IMPROVING THE CITY FOR ITS PEOPLE, BUSINESSES AND VISITORS.

When it comes to the welcome, friendliness and atmosphere people experience when visiting, Preston is proud to be on par with, if not ahead of, other much larger destinations. This is partly because it has always been loved by its own people, who work hard to promote the city's best qualities within their businesses and organisations. Preston BID is one of these organisations, which exists to support other businesses and promote the city. It is funded by businesses, and much of the work it does is governed by those organisations it represents.

The dining sector is a very important part of the whole in Preston, and the quality of independent businesses that have sprung up alongside big brands provides people with an abundance of choice. Different 'foodie quarters' have even emerged in the city, including an area now renowned for a huge range of authentic international cuisine, which serves the overseas student population as well as more adventurous locals. At the other end of the spectrum – as northern as you can get – is a pie and mash shop, which has taken root and demonstrates the longevity of Preston's diversifying culinary landscape.

Businesses across the sector strongly support each other in Preston, which is a key factor in the city's thriving and award-winning dining and nightlife. Bars and pubs recognise that restaurants and eateries go hand in hand with their offer, so people can enjoy a great evening out in all aspects. When it comes to tracking down your favourite tipple, there is no shortage of choice with everything from gin palaces and microbreweries through to traditional pubs, clubs and bars, all of which still prove very popular.

In 2019 Preston BID celebrates its tenth year and is "looking forward to working with visitors and businesses to make the next ten even better!" The last decade has seen significant evolution, and new initiatives have been put in place very recently to bolster the food and drink sector even more. The new market hall, for example, has welcomed more than half a million visitors in its first year, attracted by local produce as well as quirky street food within a modern space that nods to its Victorian roots. Preston BID is also working with Makers Market, a showcase for artisanal producers (of which the majority create unique food and drink) that began in May 2019 and will run monthly.

GOOSNARGH CHICKEN LEGS, PRESTON PARCHED PEAS, LANCASHIRE CHEESE AND LEEK SAUCE

I take my radio show to Preston regularly, and I often stand on the flag market watching people tucking into the city's greatest secret… a portion of parched peas! They've been part of life in Preston since 1773 and they were the inspiration for my recipe. I hope you enjoy it!

250g black peas

1 tsp bicarbonate of soda

4 bone-in Goosnargh chicken legs

85g butter

Salt and pepper

85g leeks, finely chopped

30g flour

570ml milk

1 tsp English mustard

115g creamy Lancashire cheese, grated

450g baby potatoes

Splash of oil

Splash of vinegar

Seasonal vegetables of your choosing

THE DAY BEFORE

Pour the black peas into a bowl and add the bicarbonate of soda. Cover with cold water, stir well, then leave the peas to soak for 24 hours.

TO COOK

Drain and rinse the soaked peas well, then put them in a pan and cover with cold water. Bring to the boil, then turn down to a simmer and cook for 2 hours, topping up the water if needed.

Preheat the oven to 150°c. Rub the chicken legs with two tablespoons of butter, then lay them in a roasting dish, ensuring they don't overlap, and season well with salt and pepper. Cover with foil, and bake in the oven for 1 hour.

Melt one tablespoon of butter in a frying pan and when hot, add the chopped leeks. Stir fry the leeks until cooked through.

Add 30g of butter to a heavy-based saucepan over a medium heat. When melted, add the plain flour and whisk into the melted butter. Stir well for 2 minutes then add a quarter of the milk and whisk well to avoid lumps forming. Once the mixture is smooth, add half of the remaining milk and turn up the heat. Whisk well, then add the rest of the milk and the mustard, and season. Continue to whisk over a high heat until the mixture turns thick and glossy. Remove from the heat, add the grated Lancashire cheese and stir well until the cheese has melted. Add the fried leeks to the sauce and stir well until combined.

Halve the baby potatoes, place them into a saucepan and add one tablespoon of salt. Cover with cold water and bring to the boil, then simmer for 20 minutes or until tender. Drain and place the potatoes on an oiled baking sheet. Using a fork, press each potato until the skin splits and it flattens. Lightly brush with oil.

Uncover the chicken and turn the oven up to 210°c. Baste the chicken legs with the juices from the roasting dish then return them to the oven with the tray of baby potatoes. Cook for 25 minutes, or until the chicken skin has browned. Check the potatoes after 20 minutes.

Drain the black peas then season with butter, salt, pepper and vinegar. Plate the peas, chicken leg, sauce and potatoes then finish with your choice of vegetables.

Preparation time: 30 minutes, plus overnight soaking | Cooking time: 2 hours | Serves: 4

NEW AND IMPROVED:
FRESH
LOCAL, FRIENDLY

DISCOVER EVERYTHING YOU NEED AT PRESTON MARKETS, WITH A VIBRANT MIX OF QUALITY, LOCALLY PRODUCED GOODS, ALL UNDER ONE ROOF. EXTEND YOUR STAY WITH A LUNCH AT ONE OF THE INDEPENDENT CAFÉS OR A DRINK IN THE REAL ALE BAR.

Having undergone an exciting major redevelopment, the new Market Hall in Preston – located under part of the grand 1875 Victorian canopy – opened in February 2018. The structure, designed to provide views up into the restored canopy, has brought the market into the 21st century while preserving its history and heritage. Traditional butchers, fishmongers, dairy and fruit and veg stalls can be found in the shape of family-run, long standing traders including Adrian Livesey's Butchers, Mark Williams Fishmonger, Superveg and Pickles of Preston. They trade alongside new food offers including Indian street food, handmade pizzas and delicious cakes.

These family-run businesses bring lots of experience along with them, leading to personable and knowledgeable service that you just can't get in the supermarket. The Market Hall is also a haven for local produce; the butchers have connections with farmers in the area and much of the fruit and veg available there is grown within Lancashire. This means the food is fresher and you can trace whatever you're buying back to its origins much more easily.

Discover a little added extra to the traditional stalls with Pickles' cheese and wine bar, where you can order a cheese and charcuterie board with matching wines. There is also an array of hot sandwiches at Redman's of Preston; why not opt for the Yorkshire Pudding Wrap, perfect for a colder day. You're spoilt for choice at lunch time with grab-and-go international street food from MoMoz paired with giant hand-made samosas.

Enjoy traditional market food at Aunty Dolly's, and a more contemporary menu including hot food, drinks and cakes at Brew + Bake and Cherry Pie. To wash it all down, head to The Orchard Bar or pick up some locally brewed craft ales from Priest Town Brewing at the Box Market, found under the historic Fish Market canopy in upcycled shipping containers. Top notch artisan coffee, tea and hot chocolate are served at Jonah's, with their wealth of knowledge finding you something new to try.

Preston Markets wouldn't be complete without the outdoor and second-hand markets. Long standing traders sell home furnishings, pet supplies, plants, flowers, clothing and gifts to name but a few. With an abundance of fresh, local ingredients, quality hot and cold food available to eat in and take away, as well as gifts and everyday items, there really is something for everyone at Preston Markets.

DELIGHTS FOR ANY TIME OF DAY...

Whether it's breakfast or brunch, snack or dinner time, Preston Markets has you covered for eating in or taking away.

BREAKFAST & BRUNCH

- Tuck into smashed avocado and chilli on toast paired with a speciality coffee, from Brew + Bake.
- Indulge with the classic traditional full English breakfast with all the trimmings, from Aunty Dolly's.
- Grab a hearty sausage barm with a Pash N Shoot smoothie to go, from Cherry Pie.

LUNCH

- Sit back and relax with a range of cheese and charcuterie boards and perfectly paired wines, from Pickles of Preston.
- If you're in a hurry, grab potatoes topped with melted Raclette.
- Try Redman's special Yorkshire pudding wrap, filled with your choice of succulent roast meat, vegetables, stuffing and plenty of gravy.
- Discover a Preston speciality with locally made butter pies from Arthur Strands.
- Create your own fresh salad box with accompanying dressing at SuperVeg.

TEA

- If you're having a barbecue, Adrian Livesey's Butchers have a wide range of burgers, sausages and flavoured steaks. Looking for something quick? The premade stir fry is ready to cook at home.
- Pick up a fresh rainbow trout caught at Fleetwood from Mark Williams' Fishmongers and pair with local fresh vegetables from Fresh & Fruity.
- Looking for something spicy? The homestyle lamb curry with fresh samosas at MoMoz is served ready to eat.
- Wanting to try something new? Just ask one of our traders for a recommendation.

PLACE THE BEERS

REDMANS
FINE FOODS

ROAST YORKSHIRE
PUDDING WRAP
with your choice of succulent roast meat,
and your favourite sauce.

REDMANS

MARK WILLIAMS
FISHMONGER

THE ORCHARD

Arthur Strand

Beef
Burgers
80p each
4 for £2.99
LIVESEY'S

Bamber's
Beef
Sausages
£2.50/lb
£5.50/kg
LIVESEY'S

Bamber's
Pork, Leak &
Black Pepper
Sausages
£2.60/lb
£5.70/kg
LIVESEY'S

WET FEET
WARM HEARTS

WHETHER YOU'RE A LOCAL OR ONE OF THE MANY TOURISTS PASSING THROUGH THE PICTURESQUE WHITEWELL ESTATE, YOU WILL ALWAYS FIND A WARM WELCOME, A STEAMING CUPPA, AND A FRESH SLICE OF CAKE WAITING FOR YOU – AND YOUR DOG – AT PUDDLEDUCKS TEAROOM.

Husband and wife Paul and Erica used to walk their dog to PuddleDucks Tearoom and dream of owning it themselves. As locals, they had always frequented the café, and given Erica's love for baking, they couldn't pass up the opportunity to get stuck into the business! PuddleDucks remains a central part of the community, housing the local post office and village shop, keeping the iconic name that locals have grown to love and hosting the friendly ducks that congregate on the lawn, but Paul and Erica have freshened up the business too with new furniture, the addition of an outdoor kiosk for takeaway food, and even more cake!

Situated at Dunsop Bridge in the heart of the Whitewell Estate – and the very centre of the United Kingdom – the tearoom offers a perfect place for cyclists, walkers, families and tourists from all over the world to take a break and enjoy the countryside. The estate is owned by the Duchy of Lancaster and has been visited by the Queen, so it's a popular destination for people as well as a renowned beauty spot. Paul and Erica welcome regulars who know them well just as

happily as passersby seeking shelter from sudden showers. With this in mind, they introduced features like free wifi and card machines and made the tearoom dog friendly to accommodate everyone.

The simple but delicious menu offers an array of homemade fare to choose from such as soups, quiches, pies and hotpots. Erica sources her produce from local suppliers, including excellent tea and coffee for a proper pick-me-up. As well as the cosy interior and sunny patio, PuddleDucks also offers food to takeaway, making for a delicious walking snack, or a family picnic at Dunsop Bridge.

Both Erica and Paul came into the hospitality industry from completely different backgrounds, but have already proved more than capable in the short time the tearoom has been reopened, with help from family members Jack, Joe and Lucia. Perhaps even more importantly, they love what they do, and they have ensured the future of their favourite place for Lancashire locals and visitors to enjoy as much as they do.

LANCASHIRE PARKIN

This parkin originated from our time living in the Middle East, when other expats enjoyed treats that reminded them of home. Our best friends, Lucy and Stephen, asked us if we would make them a wedding cake using my parkin recipe. I piped buttercream roses onto the cake which proved to be a hit, and I've made it that way ever since!

285g self-raising flour
170g soft brown sugar
140g butter
Pinch of salt
1 tsp bicarbonate of soda
2 tsp ground cinnamon
2 tsp ground ginger
½ tsp ground nutmeg
250ml water
2 large eggs
227g golden syrup

FOR THE BUTTERCREAM

85g butter
140g icing sugar
Splash of milk

Grease two 23cm cake tins and preheat the oven to 180°c.

Sift the flour, bicarbonate of soda, ginger, nutmeg, cinnamon and salt together in a large bowl. Whisk the eggs and sugar together in a separate bowl.

In a small saucepan, melt the butter and syrup with the water then leave to cool.

Add the egg and the butter mixtures to the dry ingredients and beat until smooth. Divide between the cake tins and bake for 20 to 25 minutes until risen. Use a skewer to test that the mixture is cooked in the middle. When done, turn out onto baking trays and allow to cool.

FOR THE BUTTERCREAM

Make the buttercream by beating the ingredients together with a hand mixer. Smooth the buttercream over the top of both cakes and sandwich them together.

Preparation time: 10-15 minutes | Cooking time: 20-25 minutes | Serves: 6-8

BAKEWELL TART

A longstanding, traditional family favourite prepared in our own special way.

FOR THE BASE

225g plain flour

60g icing sugar

Pinch of salt

225g butter

325g jam (Bonne Maman raspberry jam is lovely)

FOR THE FILLING

4 eggs

150g caster sugar

150g ground almonds

150g butter, melted

60g flaked almonds

FOR THE BASE

Preheat the oven to 180°c. Meanwhile, blitz the ingredients for the base in a food processor (or rub the butter into the flour and sugar by hand to get a breadcrumb-like texture) then press the mixture into a 30cm by 10cm foil tray or a lined tart dish.

Bake the base in the preheated oven for 20 minutes until golden. Allow it to cool and then spread the jam over the base.

FOR THE FILLING

To make the frangipane topping, whisk the eggs, sugar and ground almonds together. Continue to mix (this is much easier with an electric stand mixer) while you add the melted butter until everything is combined.

Pour the frangipane mixture over the jam. Use a dry frying pan on a medium heat to toast the flaked almonds, and once golden scatter them on top of the frangipane. Bake the tart until golden, for around 25 minutes.

This is delicious served warm from the oven with a scoop of ice cream, or you can enjoy a slice after it has cooled anytime!

Preparation time: 20 minutes | Cooking time: 25 minutes | Serves: 8

A CUT ABOVE

FROM FARMSTEAD TO PICTURESQUE COUNTRY INN, THE RED PUMP INN HAS BEEN TRANSFORMED INTO A DESTINATION FOR STEAK-LOVERS, GLAMPERS AND GUESTS LOOKING FOR A TOUCH OF RUSTIC LUXURY IN LANCASHIRE.

Offering a luxury B&B experience and fast establishing a fine reputation for the quality of their steak restaurant, Jonathan and Frances have restored the historic Red Pump Inn to its former glory, injecting new life and character by the bucket load. With an elegantly rural interior featuring stone flag floors, oak beams and crackling open fires, the inn has eight boutique bedrooms which have been designed with a nod to casual French elegance and thoughtfully furnished to make guests as comfortable as possible.

Recommended in Alastair Sawday's Secret Places and the Good Pub Guide, the restaurant is frequently filled with locals enjoying a seriously good steak along with mid-week visitors from throughout Lancashire, and travellers from further afield who appreciate the relaxed and informal atmosphere. The kitchen team, led by head chef and Lancashire lad Neal Waterfield, source the finest beef through award-winning butchers and specialise in native Longhorn, Shorthorn and Galloway cattle which mature slowly, developing a wonderful flavour as they graze on a natural diet of grass and hay. The steaks are then dry aged, often for over 40 days, resulting in exceptional quality cuts such as fillet, sirloin, rump, rib-eye,

picanha (a speciality rump cut popular in Argentina) and our signature steak: prime rib cooked on the bone.

In addition to creating a niche for steak lovers, The Red Pump Inn's menu has options for any foodie who loves rustic style dishes cooked with superior ingredients. It changes every six weeks and often includes classics such as Fran's Irish Stew and Fish Chowder. As a country inn, there are of course plenty of drinks to sup alongside your meal, and the new beer garden enjoys commanding views across the Ribble Valley to the legendary Pendle Hill and Longridge Fell.

Another recent addition to The Red Pump Inn also makes the most of its beautiful surroundings; guests can enjoy glamping experiences in luxury yurts which have ensuites and are followed by a full cooked breakfast at the inn. Warm hospitality in every sense is at the heart of every experience The Red Pump Inn offers, underpinned by Jonathan and Fran's ethos: "we care passionately about providing a genuine, warm, heartfelt welcome into our home for our guests and are motivated by the love for what we do and the quality of the product we provide."

DEVILLED KIDNEYS

Never had kidneys? Shame on you. Don't like kidneys? You haven't tried these yet! One dish we have been unable to take off our menu is these devilled kidneys cooked in a tangy tomato-based sauce with a slight kick at the end.

600g lambs' kidneys (or calves' kidneys)

FOR THE MARINADE

Pinch of salt and black pepper
1 clove of garlic, crushed
1 sprig of thyme
½ tsp chilli flakes
½ tsp smoked paprika

FOR THE SAUCE

Splash of olive oil
¼ red onion, finely chopped
1 clove of garlic, finely chopped
1 sprig of thyme
1 tbsp black pitted olives
1 tsp tomato purée
1 glass of red wine
4 large fresh tomatoes
¼ tsp anchovy essence

Remove all the suet fat and outer membrane from the kidneys and cut them in half lengthways, retaining the curved shape of the kidney, then place them in a bowl. Add all the marinade ingredients, cover and leave to soak for 24 hours in the fridge.

Find yourself a heavy-based pan, add the olive oil and bring to a sizzle. Throw in the finely chopped onion and sweat it with the garlic and thyme over a high heat for 1 minute or so. Turn down the heat and add the olives and tomato purée. Now add the red wine (having carefully reserved the rest to drink later with the finished dish) and simmer to reduce the liquid by half.

Next, chop the tomatoes into small chunks and add to the pan, then simmer these for around 10 to 15 minutes to soften. Finally, stir in the anchovy essence. The sauce now needs to be gently blitzed either with or in a blender gently, but stop before it starts to resemble a purée. This will keep in the fridge for a couple of days.

When you're ready to impress your fellow diners, pull out that heavy pan again and heat up a slug of olive oil. Drain the marinade off the kidneys then fry them on a high heat until just browned on the outside. Turn the heat down, add a couple of spoonfuls of sauce then simmer until cooked to your liking. We like ours just still pink in the middle, but each to their own – that's the beauty of food.

TO SERVE

Place a slice of your favourite toasted bread on a plate and place the kidneys in the centre. Quickly stir the sauce in the pan, gathering any of the burnt brown bits from the base, and pour it over the kidneys. Garnish as you wish, then pour a glass of wine, close your eyes and imagine yourself in the kind of gentleman's club where, according to Thackeray, they breakfasted on devilled kidneys at three o'clock.

Preparation time: 20 minutes | Cooking time: 5 minutes | Serves: 4 as a starter

A BUSINESS IN BLOOM

CAFÉ AT SPRING COTTAGE IS A UNIQUE PLACE OFF THE BEATEN TRACK, RUN BY A FAMILY WHOSE HOUSE AND LAND GAVE THEM AN OPPORTUNITY TO CREATE SOMETHING ENTIRELY NEW FOR THEMSELVES AND THEIR COUNTY.

In a remote village amidst Lancashire countryside, surrounded by woodland and a natural stream, Café at Spring Cottage offers freshly made food in an idyllic setting. When Judith and her two daughters, Rosie and Jennie, acquired the property it was very much a return to what they knew as the family grew up in Rivington and are part of the close-knit community there. A change of livelihood for all of them started when Jennie had a 'DIY' wedding in the grounds, and someone enquired about celebrating their own wedding there, having fallen in love with the whole aesthetic. The general feeling was 'why not' even though it was never planned to become a venue, and from that first event they soon had a dozen more booked in!

The café, which opened officially in 2016, has always been the hub of the venture. There are plans to double the seating area in 2019 because its popularity and small size are somewhat at odds! "It is hard work, but we love it," says Jennie. Rosie is the creative cook while Jennie is front of house, and decisions are made between the sisters, their mum Judith and step-dad David so it really is a family-run business in the truest sense.

"We just work really well together, and actually everyone thinks all our staff are related to us because we all love to chat and there's a real harmony between everyone; the team are our greatest blessing really."

The order of the day at Spring Cottage is always for visitors to leave happy, whether they've started married life, thrown a big party, or just popped by for a piece of cake there. Their food is central to the whole endeavour, based on an ethos that uses fresh produce from local suppliers in seasonally-inspired menus which evolve throughout the day. This effectively allows the café to serve a constant flow of homemade food without any waste, and adapt to what's around inventively. Judith reads, travels and forages to bring new ideas in and introduce new ingredients too. Through a genuine love for what they do, the family have ensured that Spring Cottage has found recognition even though they weren't looking for it, and the café is going from strength to strength thanks to the talents of everyone involved and a very special location.

Welcome to Spring Cottage

Spring Cottage

SMOKED SALMON PÂTÉ

We always try to add a fish dish onto our little menu as it always goes down a treat. A lot of the staff working for us love salmon so we decided to try out smoked salmon pâté one day, and what a delicious, creamy delight it turned out to be! It's so easy to make and one of our best sellers so this was a no-brainer when we were asked to share a recipe with you all.

200g cream cheese

1 lemon

300g smoked salmon

2 tbsp fresh chives, finely chopped

1 tbsp cress

TO SERVE

Your favourite toast or crackers

A nice helping of freshly chopped salad

Firstly, use a blender to combine the cream cheese and the juice of half the lemon together. This loosens the cream cheese ready for the salmon. Once mixed, add the smoked salmon slowly until you get your preferred consistency. Use a rubber spatula to remove the pâté and place into a bowl. Mix in the chopped chives until they are spread throughout.

TO SERVE

Top the pâté with cress leaves and eat with toasted bread or crackers, alongside a yummy salad. Super simple but super tasty!

Preparation time: 5 minutes | Serves: 4

SWEET TREATS FOR

EVERY SEASON

ANDREA RUNS SUNFLOWER KITCHEN FROM HER HOME, PRODUCING DELICATE FRENCH PATISSERIE AND LUXURIOUS CHEESECAKES WITH A LOCAL TWIST.

Sunflower Kitchen is a mobile patisserie created by Andrea, a passionate pastry chef who retrained after redundancy, willingly exchanging the career ladder for an apprenticeship in order to gain all the skills she needed to establish her own business. When Andrea fell pregnant during one of her first jobs in the kitchen, she decided that it was now or never. Just a few months after her baby arrived, Sunflower Kitchen also came into being and started to adapt and evolve based on what people enjoyed as well as the local and seasonal produce that gave Andrea inspiration.

Setting up on her own allowed Andrea the freedom to delve creatively into Lancashire's natural flavour palate, by using ingredients of the best quality with only a few miles on the clock. Anything that can't be grown in the county is sourced from nearby suppliers, which not only means that Sunflower Kitchen's produce is really fresh but has also given Andrea the opportunity to meet other small producers and learn from their experiences while sharing hers. She also changes her menus according to the season, balancing the more usual combinations with customer favourites.

Everything is handmade, from the chocolates to the meringue, and bespoke options such as large cheesecakes for a celebration can come as indulgent as you like. Sunflower Kitchen is based in the Ribble Valley and delivery is free within 30 miles for those ordering online. Andrea also takes her products to markets and events across the north-west where most people discover and buy them, and is branching out geographically as her company's reputation grows.

Sunflower Kitchen specialises in cheesecakes but also creates tarts, macaron, petit fours, sachertorte and much more. Gluten-free, vegan and diabetic-friendly options are available on request, and Andrea has recently developed a range of low-carb high-protein cheesecakes for her friends at the gym where she trains as a weightlifter. Not one to do anything by halves, Andrea's dedication and love for her craft has taken Sunflower Kitchen from seedling to bloom in a very short space of time, and is excited about the future of her growing venture, as are her many fans!

GOOSNARGH GIN AND TONIC CHEESECAKE

I always loved the idea of combining my favourite tipple with cheesecake, and when I found Goosnargh Gin the flavours just seemed perfect! The gin has hints of elderflower, meadowsweet and yarrow and after a few experiments, I hit on the perfect recipe.

FOR THE BASE

115g butter

65g caster sugar

175g plain flour

1 tsp caraway seeds

100g butter

FOR THE FILLING

5 leaves of gelatine (or 1 ½ sachets of Vegi Gel, according to packet instructions)

400g white chocolate

550g cream cheese

350g sugar

300ml double cream

2 limes, zested

50ml Goosnargh gin (or more if you prefer but total liquid should not be more than 150ml)

50ml Mediterranean tonic

25ml elderflower cordial

½ a lime, juiced

TO FINISH

100ml double cream, whipped

1 lime, sliced thinly

FOR THE BASE

Preheat the oven to 180°c. Cream the 115g of butter and the sugar together until light and fluffy, then sift over the flour, add the caraway seeds and mix with a wooden spoon until the mixture resembles breadcrumbs. Using your hands, work gently until it forms a smooth dough.

Grease a flat baking tray and line it with greaseproof paper, then press the dough onto the tray. Keep it an even thickness to ensure an even bake. Bake for around 15 minutes until the biscuit is just turning golden, then leave to cool. Break it up and whizz in a food processor, or bash with a rolling pin until it looks like breadcrumbs.

Melt the 100g of butter, then gradually add it to the biscuit crumbs, stirring all the time. You want the mixture to hold together when you push it down with your spoon. You may not need all the butter so don't add it all at once.

Grease a 20cm round deep-sided cake tin and line the bottom, then push the base into the tin, making sure you press it down firmly to form an even layer. Place the tin in the fridge to chill until the filling is ready.

FOR THE FILLING

Put the gelatine in a bowl and cover with cold water then leave to soften. Meanwhile, put the white chocolate into a heatproof bowl and set it over a pan one third full of simmering water, ensuring the bowl does not touch the water. Leave to melt, stirring occasionally, then cool slightly.

Combine the cream cheese and sugar with a wooden spoon until smooth. In a separate bowl, whisk the cream to soft peaks, then combine with the cream cheese mix, whisking together until smooth. Add the lime zest and mix well.

Put the gin, tonic, elderflower cordial and lime juice in a saucepan then bring to a simmer. Add the softened gelatine and stir to ensure it has all dissolved, then pour this mixture into the melted chocolate, stirring quickly. It will look a little lumpy at first but keep stirring! Add this to the cream cheese mixture and whisk together, then pour the cheesecake filling into the tin. Leave to set for around 2 hours in the fridge.

When set, run a knife around the edge, then push the cheesecake out from the bottom, and transfer carefully to a plate. Smooth the edges with a palette knife then decorate with whipped cream and slices of lime.

Preparation time: 45 minutes | Cooling time: 2 hours | Serves: 8-10 (generously)

NOT SO
RUN OF
THE MILL

TWELVE IS A MODERN RESTAURANT AND OUTSIDE CATERING SPECIALIST WITH AN INNOVATIVE AND SEASONALLY-LED APPROACH TO FOOD, SITUATED UNDER THE SAILS OF MARSH MILL WINDMILL IN THORNTON.

The ethos behind Twelve remains the same today as it was in 2000 when the doors first opened. Owners Caroline and Paul are still very hands on, ensuring that the delicious food and friendly service are top notch for each customer. "We have tried to build a reputation for creativity combined with a passion for great hospitality that makes people's experience here enjoyable in every aspect," say the couple. Accolades including the Michelin Bib Gourmand – which Twelve has retained since 2005 – two AA rosettes, and Taste Lancashire's Restaurant of the Year Award for 2018/19 show how successfully the business has stuck to these aims.

They have also grown an outside catering company alongside the restaurant which regularly serves up food at large scale venues and events across the county. For both the restaurant and the catering, menus are bold, innovative and focused on clean and simple flavours. The starting point is always what's available in the market, so the à la carte menu changes quarterly with the seasons and there are dishes that evolve on a weekly basis as well. Head chef Graham Floyd creates his own versions of dishes people know and love: British food with a northern twist, and draws on influences from around the world to bring excitement and above all great flavour to the table.

Twelve doesn't class itself as a fine dining establishment, because although the food and service is at that level, the team want to encourage a relaxed atmosphere with staff who are friendly and approachable. "There are no boundaries – no dress code or anything like that – because we just want people to be comfortable," says Caroline. The company has around 55 staff as a whole, and as the owners say what they produce is 'only as good as our people' so they are always aiming to exceed customer expectations in every aspect of Twelve's dining and catering experiences.

The restaurant also hosts a range of regular events from gin tastings to comedy nights that feature a pre-show supper. The idea is to offer the neighbourhood something different with a variety of options for a fun evening out. Throughout the year there's always something happening, and more recently the restaurant has opened a terraced area for guests to soak up that famous Lancashire sun and enjoy the outdoors with a drink and a nibble in hand! The combination of ultra-modern décor and the 18th century windmill which overlooks the restaurant, Marsh Mill, makes Twelve's location as special and unique as its offering.

BOWLAND BEEF FEATHER BLADE, MASH, SHALLOTS AND PANCETTA

Braised beef and mash is a firm favourite in many households. We have sourced the beef from our butcher, Clark and Sons in Catforth, and our potatoes from Sunny Bank Farm in Hambleton. The secret to this recipe is well-balanced seasoning with the use of a shallot, pancetta and sherry vinegar reduction.

FOR THE BEEF

1 medium onion, peeled

2 carrots

2 sticks of celery

3 cloves of garlic, peeled

Splash of oil

4 200g raw beef feather blade steaks (trimmed)

300ml red wine

3 black peppercorns

5 sprigs of thyme

2 bay leaves

30g tomato purée

Beef stock (stock cubes are good)

FOR THE CREAMED POTATO

1kg Maris Piper potatoes, peeled

Pinch of salt

100ml whole milk

100ml double cream

50g salted butter

FOR THE REDUCTION

3 large banana shallots

150g pancetta

50ml sherry vinegar

3 sprigs of tarragon and parsley, finely chopped

TO FINISH

25g salted butter

3 cloves of garlic

6 sprigs of thyme

Maldon salt, to season

300g seasonal vegetables

50g salted butter

FOR THE BEEF

Chop all the vegetables into roughly 1cm slices then fry them in a pan with a little oil until soft and slightly browned. Place into an ovenproof dish along with the feather blade steaks, red wine, peppercorns, thyme, bay, tomato purée and enough beef stock to cover everything. Bring to a simmer on the hob then cook in the oven at 150°c for 4 to 5 hours. Alternatively, place into a slow cooker on medium for 6 to 8 hours.

FOR THE CREAMED POTATO

Chop the potatoes into evenly sized pieces, cover with water in a saucepan, add a pinch of salt then boil until soft. Drain and return to a dry pan over a medium heat, stirring continuously to avoid sticking. Pass the cooked potatoes through a fine sieve then season with fine salt and stir in the milk, cream and butter. Transfer the creamed potato to a piping bag and keep warm until serving.

FOR THE REDUCTION

Dice the shallots and pancetta separately. Place the pancetta into a heavy-bottomed pan and fry slowly. The natural fats will come out so don't use any oil. Once the pancetta begins to crisp up, strain the fat into a bowl and set the pancetta aside. Return the fat to the original pan then add the diced shallots. Sweat until they are soft and translucent, then add the sherry vinegar. This will deglaze the bottom of the pan. Reduce the vinegar until it's almost all gone and the mixture looks like a jam. Stir in the pancetta along with the chopped tarragon and parsley.

BACK TO THE BEEF

Once the beef is cooked, carefully remove it from the cooking liquor. It should feel very tender. Reduce the cooking liquor in a wide pan by at least half. Keep checking the taste and consistency. It should start to thicken, but gravy granules or other thickening agents can be added. Strain the sauce when you're happy with the consistency.

TO FINISH

Pan fry the feather blade steaks in a splash of oil with the butter, garlic, thyme for 2 to 3 minutes on each side while continuously basting. Remove from the pan once crispy and season with the Maldon salt. Cook your preferred seasonal vegetables in the butter and enough water to cover them for 2 to 3 minutes until tender. Add the shallot and pancetta reduction to the beef sauce and plate everything as pictured.

Preparation time: 45 minutes | Cooking time: 4-5 hours | Serves: 4

STRAWBERRY AND WHITE CHOCOLATE CHEESECAKE WITH DANDELION AND BURDOCK

This dessert doesn't look like a classic cheesecake, however it has all the trademark textures. We have used various techniques and flavours to create this heavenly plateful!

FOR THE DANDELION AND BURDOCK GEL

400ml dandelion and burdock cordial

5g agar

FOR THE VANILLA CHEESECAKE MIX

1 vanilla pod

300g soft cream cheese

60g icing sugar

200ml double cream

FOR THE GRANOLA

25g flaked almonds

25g oats

10g poppy seeds

15g sunflower seeds

15g pumpkin seeds

30ml Lancashire honey

FOR THE CARAMELISED WHITE CHOCOLATE

70g white cooking chocolate

TO FINISH

400g strawberries

FOR THE DANDELION AND BURDOCK GEL

Bring the dandelion and burdock cordial and agar up to a vigorous boil over a high heat. Whisk and continue to boil for 1 minute. Pour the liquid into a container and set in the fridge. Once it has set hard, blend the jelly until smooth. This is called a fluid gel. Set aside until plating up. You can simply portion the set jelly into cubes if you don't have a blender.

FOR THE VANILLA CHEESECAKE MIX

Split the vanilla pod in half lengthways and scrape out the seeds. Beat these with the cream cheese and icing sugar until combined. Gradually pour in the double cream and whisk until the mixture is a smooth piping consistency. Pass this through a sieve to remove any lumps, then spoon into a piping bag.

FOR THE GRANOLA

Mix together all the dry ingredients then stir in the honey. Spread this mixture onto a tray lined with baking paper and bake in the oven for 15 minutes at 160°c. Stir at 5 minute intervals to prevent burning around the edges. When done, cool then store the granola in an airtight container. This is ideal to have in the cupboard for future use; it goes really well with any fruit or sprinkled into yoghurt.

FOR THE CARAMELISED WHITE CHOCOLATE

Line an oven tray that's small enough to fit in your fridge with baking paper. Break up the white chocolate on the tray and bake in the oven at 160°c for 10 to 12 minutes until golden brown. Leave the tray to cool on the side before placing it into the fridge so the chocolate sets. Smash up the chocolate into a crumble.

TO FINISH

Prepare the strawberries by rinsing and taking off the stem, then cut into bite-size pieces. Lancashire summer strawberries are our preferred choice. If your strawberries aren't sweet or ripe enough then soak them in a little sugar syrup for 5 to 10 minutes before serving. Pipe the cheesecake onto the plate, add a few dots of the dandelion and burdock gel then arrange the prepared strawberries as pictured. Finally throw on a generous handful of granola and caramelised white chocolate.

Preparation time: 40 minutes | Serves: 4

THE HUB
OF THE
WHEEL

THE VILLAGE TEAROOM AT WHEELTON HAS BECOME – AS ITS NAME
SUGGESTS – A REAL HUB FOR THE COMMUNITY AND A PASSIONATE
ADVOCATE OF FRESH, HOMEMADE, LOCAL FOOD.

In 2015 Martyn and Jackie made their vision, and Jackie's lifelong dream, of running their very own tearoom a reality. The husband and wife team established their venture in the small picturesque village of Lower Wheelton, near Chorley, and called it The Village Tearoom at Wheelton to convey how important the connection to their location was. They have a strong bond with the community and regularly get involved with village events. "We wanted our customers to feel at home here," says Martyn, "and always be assured of a friendly and welcoming greeting."

Part of this ambience is due to the modern and elegant surroundings customers can enjoy. The tearoom was originally set up over two floors, but was expanded in early 2017 by the transformation of the previously unused basement into another dining area. There's also outside seating in a back courtyard and paved front space: both fantastic for al fresco feasting, especially since eco decking was laid in the courtyard to rejuvenate the space.

The tearoom is the perfect meeting place for friends old and new, whether that's over a hot drink and a slice of homemade cake, a wholesome soup and sandwich or one of their signature 'picnic basket' afternoon teas. All the food served on the tearoom's menu is freshly prepared daily on site, which is a matter of great pride for the owners and their team of 12. The open kitchen was purposefully designed so customers can see their breakfast or lunch being carefully and lovingly prepared, and many enjoy having recipe discussions with Jackie and the kitchen team. "We will try our best to cater for any type of dietary requirement at any time; it is always a pleasure to oblige and never a chore!" says Jackie.

Fresh milk, cream and free-range eggs are the most important ingredients, particularly when it comes to baking all the cakes, biscuits, pastries, desserts and scones to make up an irresistible display each morning. Because of this, all the milk and cream is provided by the local dairy farmer at Denham Springs – less than half a mile from the tearoom – and the eggs are delivered weekly from Staveley's in Coppull. Part of the tearoom's mission is to support Lancashire suppliers, all of which are proudly listed on the back of the menus. Martyn and Jackie would love The Village Tearoom at Wheelton to become your perfect excuse for an enjoyable treat with family or friends.

ROASTED PEPPER
AND COURGETTE SOUP

Having an abundance of freshly home grown peppers and courgettes one day, we created this simple recipe, packed full of nutritional goodness and wonderful home grown flavours.

1 medium onion

1 medium leek

1 green pepper

1 yellow pepper

1 red pepper

2 medium courgettes

1 clove of garlic, crushed

60ml vegetable oil

1 litre water

2 tbsp vegetable boullion

Ground black pepper

Chop the onion, leek, peppers and courgettes then sauté them together in a large saucepan with the crushed garlic and vegetable oil. When vegetables have slightly softened, add approximately 1 litre of water (you might have to add a little more if the water evaporates too quickly). Stir in the vegetable bouillon and then leave to simmer for around 15 to 20 minutes.

When the soup is cooked, either blend with a hand blender or pour into a large heatproof blender and blend. Finally, taste and season accordingly with black pepper.

Best served with rustic bloomer bread and the best butter you have!

We also serve this soup at The Village Tearoom at Wheelton as part of our 'soup and a sandwich' offer, and it's a favourite with our customers as the 'soup shot' of choice in our afternoon tea picnic baskets.

Preparation time: 5 minutes | Cooking time: 15-20 minutes | Serves: 6

GETTING

HANDS
ON

KEEP IT SIMPLE IS THE HEADLINE RULE AT WE DON'T GIVE A FORK, WHICH
SELLS THE BEST BURGERS IN PRESTON AND NOTHING ELSE BESIDES.

In 2017 Mark O'Rouke established a burger bar in a small venue with enough seating for 34 diners over a basement and ground floor. This unassuming venture took burger fans by storm, thanks to the owner's premise which is that when you only do one thing, you can do it exceptionally well. We Don't Give A Fork offers, as its name suggests, a super casual dining experience where no cutlery is needed and getting messy is all part of the joy.

Mark had always wanted to open his own restaurant, but when the opportunity arose to buy his own premises, he knew the space wouldn't suit sit-down dining, so instead he made burgers the sole focus of We Don't Give A Fork and put all his passion and experience into making them great. This starts with the ingredients, of course, so the patties went through an extensive development phase before the business even opened its doors. 100 burgers later the combination of rib, topside and chuck proved the perfect formula for both consistency and taste in a classic beef burger.

This is all sourced from the city centre's closest farm, and complemented by market produce that varies depending on the season. It's very important to Mark that his chefs are using the best quality they can get, which always means matching the time of year for freshness and the fullest flavour. Having previously worked in both cheffing and management, Mark has written and executed menus from both sides of the pass so uses that industry knowledge to make Fork's burger top notch.

Today there are five patties to choose from which can be paired with any of the four types of bun, ten cheeses and ten sauces on the menu alongside five house specials for the less decisive. These will incorporate flavours from all over the world — mozzarella and basil for Italy, chorizo and peppers from Spain — but also cater to allergies and intolerances so everyone can indulge.

The burger bar has recently launched a catering trailer, bringing these tastes to more people at events such as weddings and festivals. Summer 2019 saw its first outing, and the plan is to continue spreading the burger love in Preston and beyond with We Don't Give A Fork's no nonsense attitude to chowing down.

LAMB BURGER WITH TZATZIKI, ROASTED PEPPERS AND HALLOUMI

Chef's tip: for a juicy burger, only ever flip a patty once and never press it down during cooking as that lets the juices escape. If you have any chili jam knocking about this can add another dimension to the layers of flavour in the finished burger.

FOR THE BURGERS

800g minced lamb (from the butcher)
3 tbsp chopped fresh rosemary
1 tbsp ground garlic
1 tbsp Dijon mustard
Salt and pepper
1 pack of halloumi, sliced

FOR THE TZATZIKI

150g Greek yogurt
½ a cucumber, diced
4 cloves of garlic, crushed
1 tbsp virgin olive oil
1 tbsp white wine vinegar
½ tsp salt
½ tsp white pepper

TO ASSEMBLE

4 top quality brioche buns
1 red onion, sliced
Handful of spinach leaves
1 red pepper, roasted

FOR THE BURGERS

Mix the lamb, rosemary, garlic and mustard together then divide into four and shape into large patties. Don't handle the meat too much as this will toughen it. Refrigerate the patties for at least 1 hour. This helps firm them up so they don't fall apart when cooking.

FOR THE TZATZIKI

Meanwhile, put all the ingredients for the tzatziki in a bowl and stir well to combine. Leave in the fridge until ready to assemble the burgers.

When the patties are chilled and you're ready to cook, season both sides with salt and pepper then fry or grill them over a really high heat until cooked. 3 or 4 minutes per side should do. Fry or grill the sliced halloumi at the same time.

TO ASSEMBLE

Put a generous dollop of tzatziki on the bun bases, then add red onion and spinach leaves followed by the burger patties, halloumi slices and a quarter of the roasted pepper each. Finish off with another dollop of tzatziki then get stuck in.

Preparation time: 10 minutes | Cooking time: 10 minutes | Serves: 4

ONE

IN A MILLION

OPENED AS PART OF A £12.9 MILLION PROJECT, WILFRED'S RESTAURANT
AND BAR IS A STANDALONE LUXURY VENUE BESIDE CROW WOOD HOTEL
WITH A STATE-OF-THE-ART £1 MILLION KITCHEN.

Wilfred's Restaurant and Bar opened in 2019 and is headed up by the same team behind the award-winning Bertram's Restaurant and The Woodland Spa. With a nod to an Italian theme, Wilfred's is a family-friendly restaurant with an extensive children's play area to keep the little ones busy while parents relax and enjoy the food on offer. Spencer Burge and his team of dedicated chefs produce an eclectic offering to excite the whole family. From local grass-fed aged steaks and Mediterranean-style fish dishes to stone baked pizza and handmade steak burgers, there is plenty of choice on offer to keep the local community and hotel guests coming back for more.

Crow Wood Hotel sits in 40 acres of beautiful Lancashire countryside, boasting an enviable backdrop of the famed Pendle Hill. Gorgeous grounds look out into the surrounding woodland, providing a picturesque setting for weddings and events, with an ornamental lake and gardens, and the meandering River Calder close by. The landscape ensures a stunning setting in every season, with bluebell woods in spring, wildflower meadows in summer and even snow-capped hills in winter.

The array of flora and fauna in the grounds also attracts an abundance of wildlife and, if you wake up early enough, you might catch a glimpse of wild deer wandering through the grounds and the resident kingfisher hovering above the lake. Six luxury executive suites on the top floor of the hotel have extensive views over the countryside across to Pendle Hill and sumptuous décor…with all that in mind you might not want to leave your room, but the lure of delicious food and drinks in Wilfred's Bar and Restaurant might just tear you away!

With the global award-winning Woodland Spa and the Crow Wood Leisure Centre adjacent to the restaurant, you can take a thermal spa journey, hit the gym, or set off on one of the many jogging trails within the grounds. Or, you may just want to sit and soak up the countryside views sipping a cocktail or two on the hotel veranda. Whatever your tastes, this luxury resort at the heart of the Pennine Lancashire countryside has it all.

JAMBALAYA ARANCINI

Jambalaya is a dish that originated in Louisiana with Spanish, French and West African influences. Turning this flavourful one pot meal into arancini – Italian deep fried risotto balls – is a great way to enjoy food fusions and makes a great starter or canapé.

250g smoked Spanish chorizo sausage

250g chicken breast

150g red pepper

150g green pepper

150g yellow pepper

1 red onion

25ml pomace oil

½ tsp paprika

½ tsp turmeric

½ tsp garlic purée

250g Arborio rice

550ml hot vegetable stock

1g saffron threads, soaked in 20ml warm water

10 spring onion, finely sliced

100g cooked prawns, chopped

100g flour

2 eggs, beaten

300g breadcrumbs

Dice the chorizo, chicken, peppers and onion into small cubes. Fry the chorizo in a pan with the pomace oil on a medium heat, then once the chorizo has let all its oils bleed out, add the chicken, onions and peppers. Continue to cook for 3 minutes then add the paprika, garlic and turmeric and stir well. Add the rice, half of the vegetable stock and the saffron threads as well as the water they were soaked in. Stir everything well and continue to cook the rice, adding more warm stock as you go along, until it has absorbed most of the liquid and is just done.

1 minute before taking the pan off the heat, season to taste and add the spring onion.

Spread the mixture thinly on a tray to cool then leave in the fridge. When the mixture is cold, add the prawns and mix well. Form into 45g balls and place back into the fridge to firm up.

Coat the balls in flour, beaten egg and then breadcrumbs. Do this carefully to get a good shape on each one. Deep fry the arancini in oil until golden brown, then finish in the oven at 170°c for 3 to 4 minutes just before serving.

Preparation time: 20 minutes | Cooking time: approximately 40 minutes | Serves: 8 as a starter

THE
SAUSAGE
SPECIALISTS

TRADITIONAL BUTCHERY MEETS SPECIALITY AND INNOVATION
AT YE OLDE SAUSAGE SHOP IN OSWALDTWISTLE MILLS.

Ye Olde Sausage Shop was established in 2006 by Martin and his father-in-law David. His brother-in-law later joined the business, and his cousin Jessica, who started as a Saturday girl, is now a partner in the family-run business. With a fairly small team, the shop is a traditional butchers but has always specialised in other products including the wide range of gourmet sausages that have been recognised with lots of local and national awards and more recently the fancy stuffed chicken, pork and pastry products. The Slimmer's Choice Fat Free Range has also grown extensively over the past decade.

Produce is sourced from within the county where possible. All pork comes from the Bowland Forest area and the award-winning Real Lancashire Black Pudding Company are a regular supplier. The shop has a minimum of twelve flavours of sausage available daily, as well as gluten-free options with products collected locally or ordered online. Alongside steaks, joints, chops and usual cuts, Ye Olde Sausage Shop sells ready-made food such as casseroles, curries, stir fries and more that can go straight from the counter to the oven at home.

Customers can see products being prepared behind the counter, including the butchery and sausage making. With a member of Team GB in the family there are plenty of skills on display too! Jessica was the first woman to represent Great Britain in Butchery in the World Butchers' Challenge, in which she competed in 2018. She will be staying on the team for the next challenge in 2020 in Sacramento, California. Learning from these competitions allows Jessica to bring ideas and skills back to the business from all over the world, as she competes alongside butchers from almost every country.

These inspirations and the shop's unique location have enabled the business to diversify and create the unusual products that are loved by regular customers and interest new customers. Oswaldtwistle Mills is a shopping centre with food hall, with the counters and preparation areas centre stage. Ye Olde Sausage Shop uses this space to best effect with eye-catching displays and occasional events focusing on a particular product which are advertised on social media, an important part of the fan base. With over 65 years of butchery experience between its proprietors, Ye Olde Sausage Shop can proudly lay claim to its name, but there is also much more to it than the signature products!

SOME OF OUR SPECIALITIES

A small insight into some of the innovative products that we make, which collectively make up our bright, colourful and eye-catching daily display! They're all specially designed to provide our customers with quick, easy and tasty meal ideas as the majority of them can be cooked within 30 to 40 minutes, without compromising on flavour.

BLACK PUDDING AND HALLOUMI STACKS

Locally sourced black pudding from the Real Lancashire Black Pudding Company is sandwiched with halloumi and wrapped in maple cured streaky bacon. The finishing touch is to brush the stack with a sea salt and Lampong pepper oil.

Cooking Suggestion: wrap the stacks in foil and bake in a preheated oven at 180°c for 30 to 35 minutes, opening the foil parcel half way through to crisp up the bacon around the edges.

LATTICE CHICKEN

Chicken breast with chorizo and peppercorn sauce is wrapped in a lattice of puff pastry, brushed with a sea salt and Lampong pepper oil and sprinkled with pink peppercorns.

Cooking Suggestion: wrap the lattice in foil and bake in a preheated oven at 180°c for 30 to 35 minutes, opening the foil 15 minutes before the end to brown the puff pastry top.

CHIMICHURRI MEATLOAF

A finalist in the Great British Butcher Awards 2019! This pork and beef meatloaf has a chimichurri sauce centre and is topped with a lattice of puff pastry then brushed with a sea salt and Lampong pepper oil.

Cooking Suggestion: wrap the meatloaf in foil and bake in a preheated oven at 180°c for 30 to 35 minutes, opening the foil for the last 15 minutes to brown the pastry.

Preparation time: 15 minutes | Cooking time: 40 minutes | Serves 4

DIRECTORY

THESE GREAT BUSINESSES HAVE SUPPORTED THE MAKING OF THIS BOOK;
PLEASE SUPPORT AND ENJOY THEM.

BATCH DISTILLERY

Unit 10 Habergham Mill
Coal Clough Lane
Burnley
BB11 5BS
Telephone: 01282 701473
Website: batchbrew.co.uk
*Batch is a micro distillery committed to producing innovative,
premium craft spirits.*

BAY HORSE INN

Bay Horse
Ellel
Lancaster
LA2 0HR
Telephone: 01524 791204
Website: www.bayhorseinn.com
*Welcoming country pub-restaurant with a reputation for
delicious food.*

THE BEE CENTRE

Preston
Lancashire
Telephone: 01772 494487
Website: www.TheBeeCentre.org
*Creating a buzz about bees, The Bee Centre is the home of
sustainable beekeeping in the UK, a centre of excellence for bee-
related education and a producer of award-winning honey.*

BERTRAM'S RESTAURANT

Crow Wood
Royle Lane
Burnley
BB12 0RT
Telephone: 01282 471930
Website: www.bertramsrestaurant.com
*Sophisticated contemporary dining in a beautiful setting with
views of the Lancashire countryside.*

BRINDLE DISTILLERY

Holmes Farm
Sandy Lane
Brindle
Lancashire
PR6 8LZ
Telephone: 01772 323313
Email: info@brindledistillery.co.uk
*Family-run distillery that offers tours, workshops and a public
bar. Home of the award-winning Cuckoo Gin range.*

BROWNS THE BUTCHERS & THE LANCASHIRE HAGGIS CO

7 Market Place
Chorley
Lancashire
PR7 1DA
Telephone: 01257 276515
Website: www.brownsthebutchers.co.uk / www.
Lancashirehaggis.co.uk
Social Media: Find us on Facebook and Instagram
@brownsthebutchers @Lancashirehaggis
*Family-run butchers supplying locally sourced meats, and the
home of 'Lancashire Haggis'.*

BUTLERS FARMHOUSE CHEESES

Wilson Fields Farm
Inglewhite
Preston
Lancashire
PR3 2LH
Telephone: 01772 781500
Website: www.butlerscheeses.co.uk
Famous for a range of farmhouse speciality cheeses including Blacksticks Blue, handmade with milk from the family herds and surrounding farms in rural Lancashire.

THE CARTFORD INN

Cartford Lane
Little Eccleston
Preston
PR3 0YP
Telephone: 01995 670166
Website: www.thecartfordinn.co.uk
17th century inn on the River Wyre known for its high quality food, individuality and eclectic feel.

CHOC AMOR LTD

Studio 8
Cedar Farm Galleries
Back Lane
Mawdesley
L40 3SY
Telephone: 01704 822633
Website: www.chocamor.co.uk
Choc Amor is a multi-award-winning Lancashire-based manufacturer, retailer and wholesaler of fiendishly good chocolate.

CLITHEROE FOOD FESTIVAL

Clitheroe Town Centre
Lancashire
BB7 2RA
Telephone: 01200 414581
Website: www.clitheroefoodfestival.com
A one day foodie festival in the heart of historic Clitheroe with a focus on Lancashire provenance.

COWMAN'S FAMOUS SAUSAGE SHOP

13 Castle Street
Clitheroe
Lancashire
BB7 2BT
Telephone: 01200 423843
Website: www.cowmans.co.uk
Family-run butcher's shop with a range of over 75 top quality sausages.

ENCORE

Brewers Print Building
Peter Street
Chorley
PR72RP
Telephone: 01257 367357
Website: www.encorechorley.com
Contemporary British dining in a vibrant, relaxed setting with warm, attentive service.

EXCHANGE COFFEE COMPANY

24 Wellgate
Clitheroe
Lancashire
BB7 2DP
Telephone: 01200 442270
Website: www.exchangecoffee.co.uk

EXCHANGE COFFEE COMPANY

13-15 Fleming Square
Blackburn
Lancashire
BB2 2DG
Telephone: 01254 54258
Email: info@exchangecoffee.co.uk
Coffee roaster and tea merchant where you can watch your coffee being roasted and enjoy your brew in a Victorian coffee house.

FINO TAPAS

St Wilfrid Street
Preston
PR1 2US
Telephone: 01772 561655
Website: www.finotapas.co.uk
Modern Spanish Tapas.

FREEMASONS AT WISWELL

8 Vicarage Fold
Wiswell
Clitheroe
Lancashire
BB7 9DF
Telephone: 01254 822218
Website: www.freemasonsatwiswell.com
Located in the beautiful Ribble Valley, The Freemasons at Wiswell is an award-winning gastropub with rooms, providing the welcoming ambience of a pub alongside refined tasting menus and traditional pub food, created by renowned chef owner Steven Smith using seasonal ingredients and the best local produce.

THE GREEN MAN AT INGLEWHITE

Silk Mill Lane
Inglewhite
Preston
PR3 2LP
Telephone: 01995 643439
Website: www.thegreenmanatinglewhite.co.uk
Country pub known for homemade pies, views of Beacon Fell and the friendliest welcome for all the family, including the dog!

HOLMES MILL

Greenacre Street
Clitheroe
Lancashire
BB7 1EB
Telephone: 01200 407111
Website: www.holmesmill.co.uk
Spectacular food and drink, lifestyle and leisure destination at the heart of the Ribble Valley.

LANCASTER BARN B&B

Bay Horse
Lancaster
LA2 0HW
Telephone: 08443 578905
Website: www.lancasterbarn.co.uk
Unique B&B in Lancaster. All the comfort and personal touches of a B&B, but with the amenities, design and flair of a hotel. Located in the best spot for country pursuits and city pleasures alike. Follow us on Instagram @lancasterbarn

THE LARDER

50 Lancaster Rd
Preston
PR1 1DD
Telephone: 07718 901813
Website: www.larder.org.uk
Find us on Facebook @thelarderLancashire and Twitter @larderlancs and Instagram @larder_lancs
Social enterprise in Preston with a café promoting food that's healthy, local, seasonal and zero waste.

MR FITZPATRICK'S

Units 7 and 8
The Courtyard
Grane Road
Haslingden
Lancashire
BB4 4QN
Telephone: 01706 230549
Website: www.mrfitzpatricks.com
British heritage brand producing premium botanical cordials.

THE NOWT PONCY FOOD COMPANY

1225 Burnley Road
East Water
Rossendale
Lancashire
BB4 9QS
Telephone: 07966 637620 / 07971 047817
Website: www.nowtponcy.co.uk
Using fresh herbs, the best ingredients and no nasty stuff to make healthy, delicious and versatile sauces.

OTTER'S POCKET ALE HOUSE

Winckley Street
Preston
PR1 2AA
Telephone: 01772 563797
Website: www.otterspockets.co.uk
Cosy ale house with freshly made food.

THE PLOUGH RESTAURANT & BAR

2 Broadfield
Oswaldtwistle
Lancashire
BB5 3RY
Telephone: 01254 232260
Find us on Facebook @theploughrestaurant and Instagram @theplough.oswaldtwistle
Friendly and welcoming family-run restaurant and bar serving high quality dishes from gastropub classics to modern British à la carte.

THE PORT OF LANCASTER SMOKEHOUSE

West Quay
Glasson Dock
Lancaster
LA2 0DB
Telephone: 01524 751493
Website: www.lancastersmokehouse.co.uk
Family-run business producing award-winning gourmet smoked foods.

PRESTON BUSINESS IMPROVEMENT DISTRICT (BID)

9/10 Eastway Business Village
Olivers Place
Fulwood
Preston
PR2 9WT
Telephone: 01772 653000 (Option 1)
Website: www.lancschamber.co.uk
Find us on Twitter @bidpreston
Preston BID represents, supports and promotes contributing businesses in Preston city centre. Its work is funded by the businesses it represents and its principal aims are to improve appeal, safety, security and vibrancy.

PRESTON MARKETS

Earl Street
Preston
PR1 2JA
Telephone: 01772 906048
Website: www.prestonmarkets.co.uk
Sample fresh Lancashire produce, enjoy a spot of lunch, and sip craft gin or ale at the Market Hall and Box Market, before searching out a bargain on the outdoor and second-hand markets.

PUDDLEDUCKS TEAROOM

Dunsop Bridge
Clitheroe
BB7 3BB
Telephone: 01200 448241
Website: www.puddleduckscafe.co.uk
Countryside tearoom offering a warm welcome, a steaming cuppa, and a freshly baked slice of cake for you and your four legged friends.

THE RED PUMP INN

Clitheroe Road
Bashall Eaves
Clitheroe
Lancashire
BB7 3DA
Telephone: 01254 826227
Webmail: www.theredpumpinn.co.uk
Elegant country inn serving real ale and specialising in dry-aged steaks and rustic provincial food. Offers a luxury B&B, glamping yurts and a beer garden with rural views.

CAFÉ AT SPRING COTTAGE

Rivington Lane
Rivington Village
Horwich
BL67SB
Telephone: 01204 772920
Website: www.springcottage.org
A happy haven to while away the hours over a warming cup of coffee, delicious food and tasty cakes in a family atmosphere, with kindness at the centre of everything we do.

SUNFLOWER KITCHEN

Telephone: 07528 844625
Website: www.sunflowerkitchen.co.uk
Email: info@sunflowerkitchen.co.uk
Mobile home-based patisserie selling unique, handmade desserts using Lancashire produce. Free delivery to PR and BB postcodes, further afield priced on distance.

TOTI – TASTE OF THE INN

The Cartford Inn
Cartford Lane
Little Eccleston
Preston
PR3 0YP
Telephone: 01995 670166
Website: www.thecartfordinn.co.uk
TOTI is The Cartford Inn's on-site delicatessen which sells quality local produce and homemade goods, as well as serving light lunches overlooking a picturesque river view.

TWELVE RESTAURANT AND LOUNGE BAR

Marsh Mill Village
Thornton Cleveleys
Lancashire
FY5 4JZ
Telephone: 01253 82 12 12
Website: www.twelve-restaurant.co.uk
Neighbourhood restaurant and outside catering specialist serving locally sourced seasonal produce created in an innovative style. Set under the 1794 Marsh Mill windmill, the ultra-modern restaurant offers a friendly and relaxed style of service.

THE VILLAGE TEAROOM AT WHEELTON

202 Blackburn Road
Wheelton
Chorley
Lancashire
PR6 8EY
Telephone: 01254 830160
Website: thevillagetearoomatwheelton.co.uk
Friendly service and excellent homemade food at affordable prices, served in modern and elegant surroundings. The perfect excuse for an enjoyable treat with family or friends throughout the year.

VISIT LANCASHIRE

Marketing Lancashire
Old Docks House,
90 Watery Lane, Preston
PR2 1AU
Telephone: 01772 426450
Website: www.visitLancashire.com
The tourism and destination marketing organisation for Lancashire. Visit Lancashire is part of Marketing Lancashire and promotes the county's attractions, events, hospitality, food and drink businesses locally, nationally and internationally.

WE DON'T GIVE A FORK BURGER BAR

Guildhall Street
Preston
PR1 3NU
Telephone: 01772 203775
Website: www.wedontgiveafork.co.uk
Big, tasty, juicy, handmade burgers.

WILFRED'S RESTAURANT

Crow Wood
Royle Lane
Burnley
Lancashire
BB12 0RT
Telephone: 01282 421222
Website: www.wilfredsrestaurant.com
Family-friendly restaurant with a nod to an Italian theme, situated beside Crow Wood Hotel.

YE OLDE SAUSAGE SHOP

Oswaldtwistle Mills
Colliers Street
Oswaldtwistle
BB5 3DE
Telephone: 01254 382930
Website: www.yeoldesausageshop.co.uk
Traditional butchery meets speciality and innovation at the family-run butchers in Lancashire's shopping centre with food hall.

OTHER TITLES AVAILABLE

The Little Book of Cakes & Bakes

Featuring recipes and stories from the kitchens of some of the nation's best bakers and cake-makers.
978-1-910863-48-0

Plant Milk Power

How to create your own delicious, nutritious and nourishing moo-free milks and smoothies.
978-1-910863-41-1

Tasty & Healthy

Eating well with lactose intolerance, coeliac disease, Crohn's disease, ulcerative colitis and irritable bowel syndrome.
978-1-910863-36-7

Vegan North Cook Book

A celebration of the amazing vegan food & drink in the north of England.
978-1-910863-40-4

Sweet Chilli Friday

Simple vegetarian recipes from our kitchen to yours.
978-1-910863-38-1

RECENT TITLES FROM OUR 'GET STUCK IN' SERIES

The Cornish Cook Book

Featuring Gylly Beach, winner of 'Best Café' in the Southwest 2018, The Rising Sun, Cornwall Life's Pub of the Year and Edie's Kitchen run by Nigel Brown.
978-1-910863-47-3

The Edinburgh and East Coast Cook Book

features Masterchef winner Jamie Scott at The Newport, Fhior, Pickering's Gin, Pie Not, Stockbridge Market and much more.
978-1-910863-45-9

The Glasgow and West Coast Cook Book

features The Gannet, Two Fat Ladies, The Spanish Butcher, Hutchesons City Grill, Gamba and much more.
978-1-910863-43-5

The Manchester Cook Book: Second Helpings

features Ben Mounsey of Grafene, Hatch, Refuge, Masons, Old School BBQ Bus and much more.
978-1-910863-44-2

The Derbyshire Cook Book: Second Helpings

features Chris Mapp at The Tickled Trout, Chatsworth Farm Shop, Michelin-starred Fischer's, Peacock and much more.
978-1-910863-34-3

The Cardiff & South Wales Cook Book

features James Sommerin of Restaurant James Sommerin, Cocorico Patisserie, Sosban and much more.
978-1-910863-31-2

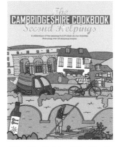

The Cambridgeshire Cook Book: Second Helpings

features Mark Abbott of Midsummer House, The Olive Grove, Elder Street Café and much more.
978-1-910863-33-6

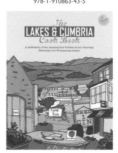

The Lakes & Cumbria Cook Book

features Simon Rogan's L'Enclume, Forest Side, Hawkshead Relish, L'al Churrasco and much more.
978-1-910863-30-5

The Nottingham Cook Book: Second Helpings

features Welbeck Estate, Memsaab, Sauce Shop, 200 Degrees Coffee, Homeboys, Rustic Crust and lots more.
978-1-910863-27-5

The South London Cook Book

features Jose Pizzaro, Adam Byatt from Trinity, Jensen's Gin, LASSCO, Salt and Pickle, Chadwicks and much more.
978-1-910863-27-5

All our books are available from Waterstones, Amazon and good independent bookshops.
FIND OUT MORE ABOUT US AT WWW.MEZEPUBLISHING.CO.UK